# Rockin' ROI:
## How to Bootstrap Ecommerce with
## Performance-based Marketing

by Jan Carroza

Library of Congress Control Number:2019950803
ISBN eBook: 978-1-7333183-0-3
ISBN Paperback: 978-1-7333183-1-0


Center for Direct Marketing
https://dmcenter.com

# Preface

## Inspiration

Initially, I was inspired by the concerns of friends, business associates and total strangers who, as small business owners, felt overwhelmed at the thought of the additional time and knowledge they needed to take on social media efforts. I knew that I wanted to help solve their problems by teaching what I've learned and sharing tools I use that save time and money. But that was just the beginning.

This project then evolved to encompass more because it also seemed like the perfect opportunity to present results-driven marketing methods, my personal passion, used by successful corporations as well as frugal-minded entrepreneurs.

## Background

I coach businesses large and small, helping with business planning, infrastructure development and marketing strategies. My client list includes brand names such as Braun, M&M Mars, Ronco, Soloflex, American Express, Volvo, QVC and Blue Cross/Blue Shield. I've also helped a lot of smaller companies find their way; sometimes in a very big way. I've run campaigns that returned $12-$15 for every $1 in media spent.

What makes me tick is my obsession to deliver the best return on marketing investment. The moment that crystallized my entire future career direction occurred early on when, as a media director at an ad agency, I prepared a plan that met all my client's goals, perfectly estimating a radio campaign to reach the target audience across several dayparts (e.g. morning drive, etc.) with the required number of average messages (frequency) and it would be under the stipulated budget. Great, right? No. My boss instructed me to go rework it to spend every dollar allowed. That just seemed wrong to me then and it still does today.

## The Bootstrap process

The upshot is an undertaking that progresses from marketing efforts that are free (or nearly free) through channels that are gradually more expensive. The chapter sequence matches the stages of a new company by covering marketing channels that cost nothing, then moving to phases attractive to bootstrapping businesses with some, but minimal funds, and finally to methods that, while they cost more, can be managed to continue to drive ROI.

## Marketing stages

No matter the budget, startups and seasoned corporations alike need to set themselves up for marketing success. The book starts with marketing goal setting and planning, moves onto the creation of a solid foundation of online and offline sites and materials and then addresses content generation to engage a target audience with built-in campaign management and measurement functionalities.

## Shifting sands

Constant changes in technology, channels and audience behaviors affect the media, marketing methods and tools available at any moment in time. From the moment of this publication, any of number of tips and tricks will become obsolete, which is why I've chosen core pillars in general use.

My hope is that readers will want to keep up with various channels that interest them, so I share the dozen or so different experts in different aspects of marketing that I rely on to learn about new trends. I have found no single source and don't presume to keep up with the myriad of changes, so I'm glad to share my go-to list. This text can only provide an overview of many choices. Once you identify your favorites, you can read the books, blogs and follow the same professionals that I would to go deeper into those topics. Additionally, I provide recommendations for further reading at the ends of chapters as well as on my blog at Dmcenter.com.

Every business will have its own custom marketing strategy that will require its unique selection of media choices. The road map for every business will continue to be a work in progress as new opportunities become available.

With a little planning, knowledge and discipline, small business owners realize they can easily manage impactful marketing campaigns on their own and dispel any concerns regarding bandwidth of time and resources.

On a final note, I want to encourage interaction. I have received tremendous support and education from experts willing to network and mentor others. Feel free to connect and reach out to me with questions. If I don't have the answers, I am glad to guide you to someone who does.

Site: https://dmcenter.com
LinkedIn: http://www.linkedin.com/in/jancarroza
Twitter: @jancarroza @dm_center
Facebook: https://www.facebook.com/Center.for.Direct.Marketing
Instagram: https://www.instagram.com/center_for_direct_marketing
Pinterest: https://www.pinterest.com/Center_for_Direct_Marketing
Email: mb@dmcenter.com

**Disclaimer**
While I may receive small commissions or other rewards for recommendations made here, I share products and services used by my colleagues or myself. As good consumers, please vet each appropriately as something written about here today may understandably not be available or of the same quality at a later date.

# Contents

# Introduction

## Profitable Marketing from Day One

### What to expect

This book is a roadmap that starts building a marketing program with free channels and tools and gradually steps into each additional effort that costs more than the last, while demonstrating how to make each one work before proceeding to the next.

This book is not: a step-by-step to implement each channel. There are many great sources for each one. What is important to me is to point people in the direction to get the best help.

I've organized chapters into three areas of activities to: 1) build a foundation and infrastructure to capture transactions, 2) create substantial, attention-getting content and 3) promote through free and paid channels and methods. I call these sections Ready, Set and Go.

The first section addresses preparations for a base camp of company and social sites to handle desired actions. This process tackles services to accept payments, ship products and manage customer service.

Additional strategies whether to do retail and International sales need to be considered, and if they make sense, when and how to launch.

Looking beyond readiness, the Set section describes activities to develop assets of interest to prospects. With basic capabilities in place to attract traffic, leads, orders and/or donations, the final Go section talks about promotion. Bootstrapping means initially taking advantage of social and other channels that are free before expanding to paid messaging.

Seven free tools and templates are included to help in business planning, budgeting, content management and results tracking. I also include some exercises to get your feet wet.

Throughout, the reader will find further suggested readings to learn more from the experts I follow and admire. Use the glossary at the end for reference to unfamiliar terms as well as a list of recommended resources. As changes continue beyond this publication, connect with current content at Dmcenter.com.

# Phase I

## Get Ready! Foundation

I mentioned in the Preface that I've seen a lot of business missteps that could have been easily avoided. This section on Foundation is meant to prevent some of those costly issues with some goal setting, decision-making, creation and set-up of assets on and off web platforms to achieve those goals.

A great foundation smoothly accommodates the activities you want your web visitors to perform, giving them a great experience, while delivering your revenue and other goals. Deciding who your target groups are, what actions you want them to take and where you want those actions to take place is key. Before building out those various web platforms, outline your consumer's process and your infrastructure to attract, nurture, close and sell again. Choose and prioritize the platforms where transactions will occur, such as web site, blog, Facebook page, etc.

### Self-assessment

By going through a company discovery process, you'll most likely identify other goals that you haven't considered yet. You might develop your Mission, Vision and Values statement, name a product line or discover another target audience. Perhaps you haven't thought about your end game.

If you intend to sell your company at some future point, realizing that goal now will define many upcoming decisions from company set-up, procedures and vendors to products and services. Plans to seek venture capital funding will also drive activities and methods you haven't thought of yet. A self-assessment exercise is included at the end of Chapter 1.

## Customer assessment

By going through a customer lifecycle process, you'll determine various touchpoints. Today's sales process isn't just point and click to buy followed by shipping. It includes consideration for the product research that consumers do, lead acquisition, nurturing and sales conversion. Customer service starts on the web site, by providing complete product and service information with FAQs. Alerts announce when products get shipped and credit cards are charged. Product boxes include a catalog or flyers to help start the next purchase cycle. Emailings ask for reviews and encourage interaction. Mapping out every step helps to create a total list of needs and activities.

## Foundation: Base camp

Once you have determined your goals and diagrammed your customer experience, your next decision is to choose the place(s) that you want actions to take place. That place or combination of places becomes the base camp and focal point of your creative efforts. Don't get lost in lazy messaging. Make it purposeful. With each creative and campaign, always remember your goals to drive your audience to your base camp.

For ecommerce-only businesses, the focus may be to drive traffic to a main site; those without a site may choose transactions to take place at Facebook or elsewhere. Just choose two initially to concentrate early efforts and gain some traction.

Retail businesses obviously want to attract customer visits to stores, restaurants, entertainment and service establishments. Web traffic is important to retailers whose prospects and clients seek office hours, product research, purchases and event details.

The important decision is to create a strategy that continually attracts traffic to the base camp group of landing pages, web and social sites.

**Key takeaway**
Good planning saves a world of hurt. Great planning smoothes the path for customers to complete the desired actions in all of the right places.

# Chapter 1

## Goal setting

### Define your business and marketing goals

When I talk to small business owners about marketing, they express concern about wasting precious time and failing to get positive results. If you set goals, map out your plan, execute well and measure results, you'll achieve success.

Far too often, marketers launch into a channel without focus and purpose. At the least, distractions from your path sap momentum and at worst, may lead to contradictions in messaging.

Think universally about the impact and changes you want to cause. How do you want to affect your customers, partners, industry and employees?

### Set Goals — Internal

**Define success** It's different for everybody. Consider what you want your marketing program to achieve. Your goals may change over time, but the initial process to think through your options not only helps you get the most out of your efforts, but it also may help you identify additional opportunities.

**Specify and prioritize** Determine everything you want to achieve. Do you want sales? Then you need leads. Do you want donations? Whether your business sells goods and services or supports the greater good as a nonprofit, the influence of social media means you must build a loyal audience of fans who share their good experiences with your organization publicly.

**List important benchmarks** Make your goals realistic, measurable and tangible. Think about long-term and well as short-term goals. For example, knowing that a long-term goal is to sell the business affects future decisions. Short-term goals set the stage for multiple successes.

Establish every possible milestone, both major and minor. Even though these goals will probably change as your business grows, preplanning reduces the pain of time and cost down the road.

## Set Goals — External

**Customers** What actions do you want from your audience? Do you want them to buy a product or service, apply for a service, register at your web site, subscribe to your emailings, refer other prospects to you, review your products and services, or support your mission? Once you think about it, there are several actions you probably want your audience to take. It's important to list all of them to facilitate choices in marketing methods. Products that cost over $100, for instance, benefit from lead generation and nurturing programs beyond a simple request to buy. If a product isn't an impulse item, it may take several "touches" or messages to secure the sale.

**Partners** Consider current and potential partnerships that could benefit you. Trusted partners offer distribution channels of loyal customers, shortening your sales cycle. Think of cross-selling, referrals and other synergistic opportunities. For example, a pastry shop might explore having coffee shops and restaurants carry their goods.

**Industry or charitable associations** Investigate the prospects that associations may offer you. Your services might be valuable to customers of companies in several industries. Conferences offer networking opportunities to develop important relationships. Public speaking and awards from your peers boost your credibility. Are there charities that are important to the mission or vision of your organization? Such relationships attract new prospects and enhance trustworthiness, integrity or authority.

## Time Management

Once you have a plan in place, you can maintain the successful, results-driven campaign with as little as an hour a day. See increased sales, lead generation and reduced marketing costs. While it will take more time initially to develop a substantial foundation, following your plan will enable you to have a manageable routine and the long-term benefits will be well worth it.

**Simplify** Your plan will help you follow a step-by-step method to systematically tackle individual parts, helping you to incrementally manage the process. Once you have completed your strategy, you'll start with the first few components that are likely to provide the most impact for the effort.

### Recommendations
Use a mind map or whiteboard to visualize your goals and the steps to achieve them. Check out Mindmeister[1] or Miro[2].

**Exercise** Explore your business needs fully with "Discovery Questions," over 200 thought-provoking queries to help you probe and define your needs and aspirations. Use them as a group exercise to survey your strengths, weaknesses, opportunities and business threats. Responses can shape business plans, executive summaries, statements of mission, vision and values, funding requests, keyword lists for names of companies, divisions, products and search engine optimization.

The exercise is several pages long, so feel free to skip it and move on to Chapter 2 to learn how to calculate how much you can spend on advertising.

---

[1] Mindmeister: Mindmeister.com
[2] Miro: Miro.com

# Chapter 1 Exercise
## Sharpen business focus through discovery

Use "Discovery Questions" to coalesce your priorities and create the most focused plan. Answers to these 200 questions help startups craft mission, vision and value statements, business plans and executive summaries, write tag lines and even carve out cornerstones, by naming an entity, its products, services or web domain. Stakeholders delve through strengths, weaknesses, opportunities and threats (SWOT), extracting and shaping concepts that provide perspective of the future.

Both nonprofits and companies benefit from an exercise to explore their essence. It isn't necessary to answer all the questions. Supporters, investors, partners, employees all have many questions of your organization. Fund-seekers must perform thorough soul-searching to present a concrete case with confidence. For all concerned, the deeper the dive, the more beneficial the process. Skip over those questions that don't apply or that you can't answer yet. Nonprofits should swap the word customer with donor.

Well-thought-out plans increase the chances to secure loans, Board Members, partners and clients. The Discovery process reveals and crystallizes the risks and rewards for everyone involved. As a work in progress, each tweak in the plan improves the outlook and smoothes the road ahead.

These questions open discussions about the problems you solve, who you solve them for, what is special about your solution, how you will make money, what you need to hit your goals and what you want to eventually accomplish.

As you go through this process, you'll develop your Unique Selling Proposition (USP), determine your strengths, weaknesses, opportunities and threats (SWOT), identify staffing needs, detail product and service lines, competition, financial projections and requirements.

While you may not be able to answer some of these questions now, considering these questions early on may improve initial planning. You may find that once deep in the discussion, your team answers early questions differently or expands more thoroughly on answers. Skip questions that don't apply.

This in-depth process also kickstarts keyword research necessary for search engine optimization of web site pages and hashtag development. Subsequently, this homework is useful for all further sales and marketing materials.

# List of Questions for the Discovery Process

## Overview
1. What does the company do?
2. What is the mission of your business and what overarching goals is it striving to achieve?
3. What does this company or project need to do?
4. Describe your mission, vision and values.
5. What are the company's long and short-term goals (what vs. how)?
6. What are the company objectives (measurable and specific)?
7. Share 5 adjectives or words that best describe your company.
8. What are the BIG ideas and 1,000-foot view concepts that speak to prospects at any stage of the buying process?
9. Why are you doing this?
10. What does success look like? Today, this year, next and five years from now?
11. How big can the company get?
12. Describe strategies (how vs. what).
13. Detail tactics (what vs. how).
14. Where are you headquartered?

## Need
15. What problem(s) do your products/services solve? What market do you fill?
16. What are the perceived benefits of solving these problems?
17. What will happen because this idea exists?
18. How will this change how people feel about x concept(s)?
19. What happens because your business or project exists?
20. How will your business help society, the environment, and any other affected stakeholders?
21. What is your business's overt benefit, dramatic difference, and real reason to believe?
22. Impact: How does your business benefit mankind?

## Unique Selling Proposition
23. What is unique about the company?
24. Why are you the people to do it?
25. What about your background, product or service sets you apart? Why should prospects engage with you and buy from you?
26. What are you really selling beyond the utility of the product or service?
27. How can you add more value?

## Revenues
28. How will your company make money now and in the future?
29. What are the revenues in the market you're targeting?
30. How big is the market opportunity?
31. How many products/services/donations must be sold to cover cost of the program?
32. Include timeline and revenue goals.
33. What are the company's requirements for success?
34. What is the timing to start? Why?
35. What are the most pressing needs or challenges that must be addressed?
36. Will you be looking for investors?

## End Game
37. What is the likely exit – IPO, M&A, sell business or other?
38. When do you see the exit happening?
39. Who will be the likely acquirers?
40. How will valuation of an exit be determined given market comparables?

## Target Audiences
41. Who are these services for?
42. Describe your ideal customer.
43. Describe your current customer if it is not your ideal.
44. Share 5 adjectives or words that best describe your customer.

45. Which groups of people are likely to be your best customers?
46. Describe customers: age, behaviors, income, lifestyle.
47. Where are your customers already looking, or not looking?
48. What have you learned from systematically talking with potential customers?
49. How has customer feedback changed your view of the business opportunity?
50. Why do users care about your product or service?
51. What product features and benefits do your customers seek?
52. What evidence convinces you that customers would buy your product?
53. What do the people you hope to serve want?
54. What do they believe?
55. How do they feel about the problem you solve?
56. Why will they care?
57. What do you want to change in the prospects' and customers' thinking?
58. What is the customer's typical day like? What issues do they face?
59. What are the customers' buying process or habits?
60. What do they do—where, when, why and with whom?
61. What will customers say to their friends to recommend this product or service?
62. How can you make customers feel good because they recommend it?
63. Where do you sell? US, Canada, Mexico? Other?
64. What is your ideal partner like? What do you want to get from them and give to them?
65. Name your industry or industries. How can you benefit from associations?
66. What publications do your customers read?

## Founders and Team
67. Who are the founders and key team members?
68. What motivates the founders?

69. Why is the team uniquely capable to execute the company's business plan?
70. How is your management team uniquely positioned to execute on this idea?
71. What relevant experience does the team have?
72. How many employees do you have?
73. What key additions to the team are needed in the short term?
74. How do you plan to scale the team in the next 12 months?
75. Who owns the development/supervision of offer configuration?
76. Identify responsible parties for fulfillment.
77. Identify who is responsible to nurture leads.

## Products and Services
78. If you sell a product, how will you distribute it? If a service, how will it be delivered?
79. How much will you charge customers for your product?
80. How much does each unit of product cost your company?
81. Which companies will supply your raw materials or key services and what are the terms of those partnerships?
82. Are your suppliers socially and environmentally responsible?
83. What are the major product milestones?
84. What are the key differentiating features of your product or service?
85. What have you learned from early versions of the product or service?
86. Provide a demonstration of the product or service.
87. What are the two or three key features you plan to add?
88. Diagram transaction flow.
89. Diagram data flow.
90. Outline customer service requirements.

## Competition
91. Defensibility: What are the barriers to entry for your competitors and new market entrants?
92. Who are your company's competitors and what are your/their competitive advantages and disadvantages?

93. Who are the company's competitors?
94. What gives your company a competitive advantage?
95. What advantages does your competition have over you?
96. Compared to your competition, how do you compete with respect to price, features, and performance?
97. What do you like about their presence? What do you dislike?

## Finances
98. What are the company's three-year projections?
99. What are the key assumptions underlying your projections?
100. When will the company get to profitability?
101. How much burn will occur until the company gets to profitability?
102. What are your unit economics?
103. What are the factors that limit faster growth?
104. What are the key metrics that the management team focuses on?

## Strengths
105. What are your assets? List types of assets.
106. Which one of those assets is the strongest?
107. What makes you better than your competitors?
108. Do you have a strong customer base?
109. What is the unique thing about your company?
110. How skilled are your laborers?
111. What special skills do your team members possess?
112. Do you have previous experience in this task (mission)?
113. What are the advantages you have over your rivals?
114. What's your greatest strength?

## Weaknesses
115. What areas need improvement?
116. What are the things you need to avoid?
117. In what areas do your competitors have an advantage?
118. Are you lacking in knowledge?
119. Are your employees skilled enough?

120. Do you have enough funding to start?
121. Is your customer base too small?
122. Are profits too small?
123. Is/are your competitor(s) miles ahead?
124. What weakness might get in the way if not addressed?

## Opportunities
125. What external changes bring opportunities?
126. What are current ongoing trends?
127. Will these trends help in a positive way?
128. Can you take advantage of the local market?
129. What is the market missing?
130. Can you provide that missing link to consumers?
131. Is/are your rival(s) failing to satisfy customers?
132. If so, can you attract those customers?
133. Will natural causes, such as weather, give you a competitive edge?
134. Is your brand name helping you to get financing?

## Threats
135. What are the negative aspects in the current market?
136. Are there potential competitors who will affect you in the future?
137. What are the obstacles you are facing in the current mission?
138. Have you done anything which may lead to a lawsuit?
139. Are your key staff members satisfied with wages and benefits?
140. Do you see staff being poached by rivals?
141. Do you see a change in consumer taste?
142. Are government regulations going to affect you?
143. How would a natural disaster affect your production?

## Marketing
144. How will you measure success?
145. What do you want to achieve through marketing?
146. How big is the market?
147. What is the addressable market?

148. How does the company market or plan to market products and services?
149. How will people find you?
150. What is the typical sales cycle between initial customer contact and closing of a sale?
151. What is the projected lifetime value of a customer?
152. How much is the average sale to a customer?
153. How long, on average, will you retain a customer?
154. How will the products be leveraged to expand the target market or gain access to new segments?
155. What impact will these products have on customers?
156. What percentage of the market do you plan to get over what period?
157. How did you arrive at the sales in your industry and its growth rate?
158. Why does your company have growth potential?
159. What does it cost to acquire a customer?
160. What advertising will you be doing?
161. How much time (per week/month/year) will you devote to marketing efforts?
162. Does the offer exist or need to be created?
163. Define the offer configuration and incentive(s).
164. What is the cost-per-order and/or ratio goal?
165. What are the goals to convert leads to sales, donations or participation?
166. Define the lead-to-sales matrix.
167. Describe the strategy, tactics, timing and expectations of sales and marketing channels.
168. Identify every source of lead/customer.
169. Diagram lead flow process based on lead qualification scoring.
170. Detail the activities at each stage of the lead process.
171. Describe the various touch activities, the sequence and timing of each to the consumer.
172. Diagram the inbound and outbound telemarketing process.
173. Share 3 links of brands whose brand identity inspires you. What do you like best about them?

174. Share 3 brands/logos that you thought were weak and what made you feel that way.
175. Using 5 adjectives or short phrases, describe your brand's desired look and feel.
176. What is the company's PR strategy?
177. What is the company's social media strategy?
178. What factors influence the target market's buying decision that might impact the key messages, such as customer environment, competitive environment, market trends, product benefits?
179. Describe inventory and lead-time requirements.
180. Describe inventory quantities to be kept on hand at various stages.
181. Describe fulfillment procedures(s).
182. List major copy points and benefits that need to be included, especially related to uniqueness.
183. Include any mandatory corporate copy, trademarks and legal copy.
184. Do you have specific guideline dos and don'ts about the colors and other elements of brand identity?
185. List marketing assets by type and quantity.
186. What, if any, coding or database changes need to be made to identify different kinds of purchases?
187. Describe current offer stuffer materials: electronic and/or hard copy.
188. Describe any stuffer materials that need to be developed, deadline and project owner.
189. Provide telemarketing scripts(s).
190. Provide telemarketing training materials.
191. Are phone numbers needed for telemarketing?
192. Is email house file included? If so, describe. What size is the house file?
193. Are you aware of any list sources?

## Traction Risks

194. What early traction has the company gotten (sales, traffic to site, app downloads, etc., as relevant)?
195. How can the early traction be accelerated?
196. What have been the principal reasons for the early traction?

## Risks

197. What do you see as the principal risks to the business?
198. What level risks do you have?
199. Do you have any regulatory risks?
200. Are there any product liability risks?

## Intellectual Property

201. What key intellectual property does the company have (patents, patents pending, copyrights, trade secrets, trademarks, domains)?
202. What comfort do you have that the company's intellectual property does not violate the rights of a third party?
203. How was the company's intellectual property developed?
204. Would any prior employers of a team member have a potential claim to the company's intellectual property?

# Chapter 2

## Marketing budget calculation

### Calculate marketing allowable

Estimate allowable funds to acquire each sale.

### What can you afford to pay?

Before you begin any marketing initiatives, figure out the amount that you can afford to spend to acquire a sale. Many businesses devote a percentage of sales to their marketing budgets. No matter how you arrive at a cost-per-order goal, the exercise to review and estimate costs kicks off an ongoing process. Use the Marketing Budget Calculator[3] to clarify costs and define the remaining allowable budget for marketing and potential profit. Do this for each product and/or bundle.

### Income versus expenses

Businesses need to price products based on a thorough examination of costs to deliver a product as well as competitive, retail and wholesale environments. Whether selling at retail and/or ecommerce, consideration for the costs of goods, credit card processing, shipping and handling, inventory storage, returns, customer service, administration and any royalties make or break business success.

### How to create marketing budget benchmarks

The Marketing Budget Calculator is used to determine revenues that can be applied to marketing. Marketers can also configure a combination of products to be sold in a bundle. The final calculation yields the allowable amount for marketing, comparing income versus expenses. The lower the cost to acquire an order (CPO) below this benchmark, the more profitable the enterprise will be.

---

[3] Marketing Budget Calculator: https://dmcenter.com/calculate-marketing-budgt/marketing-budget/calculator

Another benchmark, the breakeven ratio, compares sales to marketing costs; the goal is to achieve the largest ratio possible, greater than the breakeven ratio.

Calculate your target cost-per-order and ratio benchmarks using conservative estimates. Watch results weekly to track performance and work towards constantly improving by lowering CPO and simultaneously delivering a higher ratio.

## Sample
The template includes a sample product profile which is designed to create a bundle of products for ecommerce and/or direct response advertising where the sale of the initial product is followed by "upsells," or additional, usually related, products or services.

The assumption made in the example in the Marketing Budget Calculator spreadsheet estimates that 50% of consumers would purchase the additional product in addition to the initial offer. The total amount collected per order, on average, is $29.38. Subtracting estimated expenses from income yields $13.15. So, delivering orders for less than $16.22 generates profits. The breakeven ratio of 1.81 means that a return of $1.82 or better for every marketing dollar takes the venture in a successful direction.

Get ideas for costs to include in the Example worksheet. Then proceed to start editing and using the second blank worksheet. Begin with the retail price you have already chosen based on current competitive, retail and wholesale environments. Results of the exercise may cause you to change your retail price in the event you allow too little for marketing and/or profit.

# Marketing Budget Calculator
### Breakeven, CPO, Ratio Worksheet

| Income | Product | Upsell 1 | Combined sale |
|---|---|---|---|
| Selling price of product/upsell | $19.95 | $9.95 | $ 24.93 |
| Shipping & handling charged to consumer | $3.95 | $1.00 | $ 4.45 |
| Percentage of upsells to product sales | | 50% | |
| **Total Charged to Consumer** | **$23.90** | **$10.95** | **$29.38** |

| Expenses | Product | Upsell 1 | |
|---|---|---|---|
| Cost of finished product | $4.00 | $2.50 | $ 5.25 |
| Merchant charge (3% of total charges to consumer) | $0.72 | $0.08 | $ 0.75 |
| Actual shipping cost (per product shipped) | $2.50 | $0.50 | $ 2.75 |
| Actual handling cost (per product shipped) | $1.00 | | $ 1.00 |
| Fulfillment/customr service (per product shipped) | $1.00 | | $ 1.00 |
| Administration (e.g. 7% of retail price) | $1.40 | | $ 1.40 |
| Returns (e.g. 5% of retail price) | $1.00 | | $ 1.00 |
| Royalties (x% of retail price for producers/talent etc.) | | | |
| Telemarketing | | | |
| **Total Direct Variable Cost:** | $11.61 | $3.08 | $ 13.15 |
| | | | |
| **Breakeven CPO:** | $12.29 | $7.88 | $16.22 |
| **Breakeven Ratio:** | | | 1.81 |

Total charged to consumer minus total expenses equals breakeven cost-per-order (CPO)
Total charged to consumer divided by breakeven CPO equals breakeven ratio

Find this worksheet with built-in formulas at https://dmcenter.com/calculate-marketing-budget/marketing-budget-calculator.

Here are the steps to tackle the Marketing Budget Calculator worksheet:

1. Start by recording the retail price for your product.
2. Separately, document the amounts you charge customers for shipping and handling.
3. Insert your cost to create the finished product.
4. Write down the average shipping fee.
5. Enter the average handling fee.
6. Add your costs to process a credit card transaction; 3% of the retail price is a planning rate to use until you secure your own rate from a payment processor.

7. Estimate customer service costs.
8. If consumers call to order, add that cost as a telemarketing charge.
9. Gauge the costs of returned products. Some companies allow 5% of the product cost until they have their own benchmark.
10. Determine your administrative costs as a percent of each sale. Many firms use 7% of the product cost until they determine their actual rate.
11. Allow for any royalties, such as those offered to celebrity talent.

Once a web visitor has something in their shopping cart, recommendations for related items are important to increase the average sale, without incurring a cost to acquire them. Moreover, in-bound telemarketing results show that consumers will tolerate up to five additional upsells.

Offer configuration in direct response advertising starts with a base product with a substantial perceived value. Upsells generally are priced lower to be easy decisions for buyers. Web visitors might see suggestions for items others bought in addition to the base item.

Start with the retail price you have already chosen based on current competitive, retail and wholesale environments. Results of the exercise may cause you to change your retail price in the event you allow too little for marketing and/or profit.

The first worksheet shows an example of how a company might fill out the form. The second sheet is blank for you to use.

Nonprofits should calculate the total cost to deliver services, including administrative fees. Delivery of any premium can be calculated as a product would.

# Chapter 3

## Competitive analysis

### Know your competition

Insights drive pricing, offers, SEO and marketing strategies.

Research your market and competitors before you configure offers and decide pricing on products. This exercise is valuable to get insights that will help you close more business in less time because your research insights help you provide the best value and prices.

The Competitive Statistics spreadsheet[4] provides several suggested fields to compare company, web and social media site numbers. Hoovers, BBB.org and SimilarWeb are a few of the tools that provide company revenues, credentials and web performance statistics.

Evaluating the business figures and media elements forms a base for your marketing content and sales strategy. Reviewing features and benefits of competitors' products helps you decide how to stand apart to achieve better loyalty, growth and build a bigger pipeline of prospects.

Examples of top line business data may include revenues, credentials, number of customers, email subscribers, as well as products and employees. Study the prices, products and offers your competitors display. Free shipping with a $50 purchase is an example of an offer. Then examine competition by segment. For instance, your site may cover both diet and exercise, but one competitor may just produce exercise equipment and content. Add a field for other values that you want to analyze, such as whether competitors use surveys or polls.

Valuable web site statistics include keywords, monthly site traffic and rank, both by geography (U.S. and global) and by industry category.

---

[4] Competitive Statistics spreadsheet: https://dmcenter.com/know-your-competition/competitive-statistics

From their home pages, right click to View Page Source and look between the <head tags for their keywords used in their title and description. The average time that visitors spend on a site and the number of pages viewed per visit tell the content story of the appeal, known as stickiness. The number of links from other sites, called backlinks, demonstrates the level of interest of businesses to promote and the quantity of sites directing traffic.

Available social media metrics include followers, likes, views, subscribers and connections, depending upon the platform. As you peruse competitors' social media, take note of reviews, comments and whether each company is good at responding quickly, completely, helpfully and appropriately to customer issues.

Thorough analysis of available competitive data should provide substantial fodder to help you reduce pricing mistakes, learn new tricks you might want to adopt with your own special twist and craft a master strategy.

**Chapter 3 Exercise**
Check out your competitors' website titles and descriptions.

Go to their website and position mouse on the webpage and right click to see "View page source" on the drop-down menu. Or type view-source:domain.com in a browser.

Choose "View page source" and look between <head> tags for their site titles and descriptions to learn what keywords they may focus on. Here's an example of how it might look:

<title>Center for Direct Marketing | Performance-based promotion</title>
<meta name="description" content="Businesses can use their sites, blogs and social media practically for free to bootstrap measurable marketing results."/>

You can see that the keywords performance-based, promotion, marketing results, measurable, business, bootstrap, site, blogs and social media are important to me.

Next, look up your competition's keywords at Wordstream[5] by inserting a domain name. SimilarWeb[6] allows some searches for free to get a website analysis of any site.

**Recommended**
Neil Patel's "25 Sneaky Online Tools"[7]

Sprout Social[8] provides a free template to conduct a full social media audit.

---

[5] Wordstream: https://wordstream.com/keywords
[6] Similar Web: https://similarweb.com
[7] "25 Sneaky Online Tools" https://neilpatel.com/blog/25-sneaky-online-tools
[8] Sprout Social: https://sproutsocial.com/insights/social-media-competitive-analysis

# Chapter 4

## Call to Action

### Choosing Calls-to-Action (CTAs)
A call-to-action is a request to your audience to engage further with your organization. It might be something simple, such as asking a visitor to buy, subscribe or donate. You may, however, have a more complex sales cycle or a more expensive product/service which requires education and several communications, called touches, to secure the commitment. You probably also need to continually attract new customers to a product or service that is not an impulse buy.

### Identify your CTAs at the get-go
Deciding early on what your calls to action will be is important to minimize the time and cost of building out your marketing foundation. Going through this process will also reduce the number of changes that you make initially. Understandably, any marketing plan is a work in progress and will change as you add new products and services.

### Consider the entire prospect-proponent life cycle
Keep in mind that 88% of consumers do research online[9] before they buy, so it's important to consider all the different methods you might use to stimulate engagement. Think about your prospect's entire experience, called the life cycle, with your organization.

Your audience may visit your site during their research to learn more. They may register at your site or subscribe to your newsletter before they buy.

They may download a coupon, ebook or white paper or they may have a specific question to ask and post that through your site's contact form. In these cases, your visitors are leads for you to nurture and qualify.

---

[9] 88% of consumers do research before buying:
https://pymnts.com/news/retail/2018/omichannel-ecommerce-consumer-habits

Later, your visitors may perform the desired action, whether it's an application, registration or revenue-generating purchase or donation. Then they may become prospects again, as candidates for additional units or different products and services that you offer.

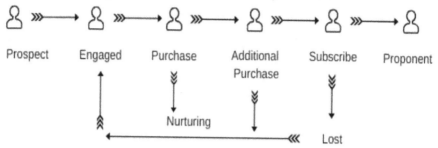

Eventually, you should ask for feedback or reviews of your goods and services. These are called "earned" mentions, basically word-of-mouth marketing, the type that 92% of consumers[10] trust more than any other, according to a Nielsen research study. Recommendations are understandably the most trustworthy type of marketing.

**CTAs determine your next steps**
The visitor actions that you choose will trigger the assets you create to capture responses. Your site, blog and landing pages will form the central core for most of your activities, however your pages on social media platforms will also provide powerful tools for collecting a wide variety of results from likes to sales. You may also use ticketing, webinar, crowdfunding or retail applications to generate sales, leads or aggregate information.

---

[10] Nielsen's "Consumer Trust in Online, Social and Mobile Advertising Grows" at https:/Nielsen.com/us/en/insights/article/2012/consumer-trust-in-online-social-and-mobile-advertising-grows

### Submit buttons are not CTAs

Some people think that the site buttons, like the one below, used to submit information, are CTAs. Don't be confused. A button is simply a tactic to have a user complete an action.

The process to determine as many possible calls-to-action as you might envision before you go further will be worthwhile. It will cause you to create assets appropriate to each and every channel that meets the needs of your plan and its CTAs, whether through Facebook, a press release or a technical publication.

### Exercise

Use the checklist to mark every interesting method you'll use to secure actions. Are there others to add to this list? You may want to sell on Amazon, Facebook and other sites as well as your own, for instance.

### Checklist

Check off every type of action you'd like visitors to perform:

- ☐ Sales on a site
- ☐ In-store sales
- ☐ Donations
- ☐ Sign-up for event
- ☐ Leads
- ☐ Registrants
- ☐ Subscribers
- ☐ Applications
- ☐ Downloads
- ☐ Reviews
- ☐ Refer-a-friend
- ☐ Request more information
- ☐ Learn more
- ☐ Other_____

### Read more

Performance of a button over a link in a call-to-action from Campaign Monitor: https://campaignmonitor.com/blog/email-marketing/2014/10/call-to-action-marketing

# Chapter 5

## Ecommerce Readiness

Now that you have discovered your goals, determined your calls-to-action and realize what cost you can afford to acquire a customer, it's time to explore what more you'll want to complete before you start marketing. Subsequent chapters cover all these steps in detail to manage everything one step at a time.

### Overview: Build your business framework

Choose vendors to make your job easier as you get ready to communicate with prospects and customers, take and ship orders. Select ecommerce, contact and email marketing platforms. Your framework must accommodate mobile users, content-sharing functionality and basic legal notices regarding privacy, terms and conditions, disclosures and compliance, such as CAN SPAM and HIPAA.

### Hosting your site

A hosting company with a website builder should accommodate ecommerce functionality and offer a choice of design themes. Make sure you choose a theme that will view correctly on mobile phones, called responsive design. Hook up your accounting, tax, email, fulfillment and other services into your ecommerce platform for ease of reporting.

### Shipping products

Amazon's Fulfillment By Amazon (FBA) simplifies life for small businesses and may make sense initially and ongoing for items sold on Amazon. Your own separate shipping center can store and ship product to support your website, affiliate and retail sales as well as ship to Amazon.

FBA takes care of inventory storage, packing, shipping, credit card processing and customer service. The big bonus is that using FBA automatically qualifies your products for Amazon Prime, which means free shipping for Prime members, accounting for an additional 10% in sales volume, plus, you'll have the boost from Amazon reviews. You aren't required to sell products on Amazon to use FBA, but if you do, make sure you create a unique offer (more in the chapter on Retail Distribution).

## Taking credit card orders
Choosing the right credit card processor, not only with the best rate, but also the most attractive terms, is important to maximize your bottom line. Additionally, review candidates for experience with retailers, ecommerce and support guidance to help prevent fraud and maintain compliance, so you can retain the privilege to accept credit card payments.

## Sending email
An email program that syncs with your contact management software, or CRM, is an essential component of your customer service, as well as your marketing program.

## Promoting with social media
Lock down the social media accounts early, even if you don't plan to put content on all of them any time soon, so you have the best chance to get the most desirable usernames, called handles. Choose a message scheduling service, such as Hootsuite to post messages for future dates. Sign up for a URL shortener, such as Bit.ly, to customize and promote content links. Create a Facebook page, secure your LinkedIn Company Profile and/or Showcase Pages for products. Often you can reserve pages and keep them private until you complete the finishing touches and publish to go live. Like URLs, the names where you invest efforts should be as consistent as possible across the networks you use.

Google is critical to your web traffic results. Get Google Analytics (free) to track your site performance. You'll need a Gmail email address for all things Google, including a Google Ads account to buy traffic, or AdSense, to post ads on your site, even if you don't plan on creating a pay-per-click campaign right away. This will give you access to

Google's Keyword Planner which will help you select your initial keyword phrases to attract traffic to your site.

## Organize your assets

While we're on the topic of setting up accounts, do it right. Keep all your business passwords safely. You can choose a software program such as Keepass. At a minimum, encrypt a spreadsheet with sign-in links, usernames and passwords, etc. Include the URL to login to the property, your username, email, password and every detail you use, such as birthdate, cell number, security questions and answers. If you lose control of a property, having every detail will help regain it. Make sure to keep these records up to date with current mobile numbers and email addresses.

Think of your domain documents as you would the deed to your home. Save these in a physical folder. I recommend printing them out and keeping them with your other important documents in a safe or safe deposit box.

Organize assets into folders. Make your logos and other images easy to find. List your company colors, fonts and marks, such as trademarks and patents. Collect your mission, vision, values statement and taglines with this corporate collection into a branding guidelines document you share within the company and with vendors, as appropriate, to maintain consistent use across activities.

## Next: Plot your roadmap and build your base camp

Decide where you want the calls to action to take place. Naturally, your web site should be the focal point for your efforts, however, you'll need to ascertain whether blog and social media pages will include buy buttons. These properties where you will drive traffic become your base camp, reminding you not to stray from focusing your efforts to make actions happen.

Then prioritize the properties and activities based on which are the most likely to perform best. This is your starting place; later you can gradually add content to more properties. Track your results so you can decide where to continue to focus your attention and that may well change over time.

Decide how you want to track those results. Begin with your benchmarks on a spreadsheet or in a software program and then regularly revisit statistics, whether weekly, monthly or quarterly.

List all important events for your business, such as trade shows, open houses, webinars, and the like, with any hashtags associated with those activities. Each convention, for instance, may have a hashtag such as #ABCExpo. Collecting this information in a format for the next twelve months, called an editorial calendar, will help you detail your plans for content development.

### Content development

Placing a conference on your calendar, for example, leads you to think about announcements as well as speaking and article publication opportunities that go into the pre-planning. Block out promotions, including event emailings prior to and post-show as well as advertising campaigns. Create deadlines for releases, articles and speech preparation. Allow time for development and approvals. Then determine participants who will share responsibility for soliciting, creating and reviewing content.

Save time by repurposing major pieces of content by editing and using new headlines, repeating important content, such as tweets about significant articles, for instance, and by scheduling content a month at a time in advance.

### Search engine marketing

Which leads us to one of the most important initial and ongoing activities: choosing the most important keywords and phrases that will draw visitors to your content. Use the Google Keyword Planner, or a similar tool, to check on terms you think of and to suggest others. The

Planner will estimate monthly traffic to those terms, helping you to select ones most likely to deliver the right audience.

Search engine optimization (SEO) is the art and science that uses the most frequently used terms across your content copy and platforms consistently to attract visitors. Start with three to five key phrases. Continue to build the list until you have ten, fifty and one hundred terms. Over the years, you may identify a thousand.

Initially, the most important phrases become a mantra that goes into your slogan, tag line, site title and/or site description. Your site title and description make up what are called your metatags. Right click on any web page to see View Source and look between these marks (</head>), called head tags.

When choosing keywords, use the strongest, most meaningful one(s) in your meta tag title, between 50-60 characters long for 90% to display properly. Here are the meta tags for Searchengineland.com:

<title> Search Engine Land | Must Read News About SEO, SEM &amp; Search Engines</title>
<meta name="description" content="Search Engine Land features daily search engine industry news &amp; trends in search marketing (SEM) - paid search advertising (PPC) &amp; search engine optimization (SEO) plus expert analysis, advice, tips, tactics &amp; How To Guides for search marketing."/>

Notice the choice of SEO, SEM and search engines keywords in the title. Meta descriptions are best kept under 160 characters to avoid truncation by the search engines. The description packs keywords together: search engine industry, paid search advertising, search marketing, spelling out search engine optimization as well as abbreviations.

The keywords used for SEO are different than those used for a pay-per-click campaign. You can use words and phrases that rank the highest for SEO, while you should choose keywords that drive the most audience for the lowest price in Google Ads advertising. Google's Planner will help estimate those ad costs. For example, a bank might use "mortgage" as a keyword for SEO but isn't likely to pay the high price to deliver clicks, which is probably over $10/click. A Nebraska bank might, however, buy a low-cost "long-tail" keyword phrase (one with several words), such as "nebraska mortgage calculator" for a fraction of the cost. So, write content using keywords that yield the greatest traffic for the best SEO results.

When you create content, whether blog posts, articles, releases or videos, consider the SEO keywords that you want to emphasize regularly as well as in each piece.

**Legal and other notices**
Several notices must be ready to post before your new site goes live. Include copyright, a privacy notice describing how you collect and use data, terms and conditions, disclosures such as a blogger disclosure regarding commissions and reference to CAN SPAM, PCI, HIPAA and other compliance, as appropriate.

**Recommendations**
Learn more about search engine everything by reading at Search Engineland, https://searchengineland.com, founded by Danny Sullivan.

# Chapter 6

## Blog

A blog gives you the opportunity to continually attract new traffic to your site with fresh content delivered on a consistent basis that demonstrates your thought leadership and often solicits a call to action. Each post helps to expand your use of keywords. Each new keyword provides opportunities to attract new visitors. Each additional use of a previously used keyword creates new breadcrumbs leading a trail back to your base camp and calls to action.

Search engines like regular, frequent, fresh content. New content helps you tap into a larger audience as you add new keywords to your blog posts, creating searchable topics. Content frequency is important. Blog posts generally cover one topic and tend to be much shorter than an article, usually 150 words minimum to about 1250 words. The concept is that readers want to capture the gist of these posts quickly. Generally, anything longer than 1250 words should become an article. Don't hesitate to write longer posts, however, to adequately cover the subject matter.

### Blog vs. newsletter

Many think they should choose between a blog and newsletter. If you have the bandwidth, I recommend doing both. Blog posts are typically about one topic, published daily and may not have a call to action on every post. Newsletters commonly are published monthly with several topics that go more in-depth, perhaps regular columns and calls to action. Newsletters get posted on the site, but most often are created to send to a list of subscribers by email. Both serve to build credibility.

If you choose to create a newsletter, enlist helpers internally and partners externally to aid in content development and give assignments. Follow your editorial calendar to provide timely references to company activities, promote free downloadable assets, request that readers forward to and refer friends. Post a calendar of trade shows and appearances, create a template to make it easy to position articles and provide fixed slots for calls to action and company information. Print newsletters out to give to prospects and clients on business calls and at trade shows.

A short version enewsletter is based on one topic in each emailing which are done more frequently, as often as daily.

## Seven keys to successful blog creation

WordPress (WP)[11], a free blog platform, makes blogs easy to set up, integrate with your URL and, for a fee, monetize with Google Ads. WP offers a wide variety of themes, or design frameworks with the choice of widgets, boxes that create structure, for instance, to enable navigation through an archive or topics. Plugins provide additional functionality ranging from SEO and backing up the blog to comment, spam management and much more.

A well-designed blog: 1) attracts traffic, 2) is easy to navigate, 3) provides credibility, 4) closes business, 5) nurtures prospects, 6) shares content easily and 7) incorporates measurement.

## 1. Attract an audience

To draw new visitors to your site, take advantage of several basic blog techniques: 1) keywords, 2) metatags, 3) blog post tags and 4) publishing posts to social media.

## 2. Create easy navigation

Make use of options to create tabs and other structural devices, such as widgets and plugins, to help your visitors easily and quickly find content and contact information on your blog. Assigning each post to a category allows readers to see several posts on the same topic. Using a widget for a search box permits keywords to steer your audience to a collection of posts.

---

[11] WordPress site to build a free blog: https://wordpress.com

### 3. Increase credibility

Embrace a commitment to create regular, thoughtful assets. Perhaps plan a quarterly white paper on topics that align with goals. Create videos, record webinars and tackle spur of the moment responses to current events, such as legislation, to let your audience know your opinion and recommend actions.

### 4. Close business

At the end of the day, capturing leads, obtaining donations and sales are the raison d'être for all the content planning and execution activities. While the blog provides thought leadership to gain credibility, it's other unforgettable focus must be to persuade and request action.

### 5. Nurture prospects

A blog and newsletter offer the opportunity to touch an audience with frequency so that when they are ready to buy, they have a warm, fuzzy feeling in choosing a company they have come to trust. The greater the cost of a product or service, the more touches that will be required to close business. Regular communication in whatever venues prospects prefer is worth the time and cost to develop relationships that close deals.

### 6. Share blog content

Provide sharing buttons and links so that prospects and customers may share content with their colleagues who may be decision-makers and new prospects. Make word-of-mouth and referrals easy because not only is there no cost to acquire that contact, but also that touch is the most powerful kind when it comes from a trusted party.

### 7. Publish posts elsewhere

WordPress and other publishing platforms offer simple ways to post your content on your other social media sites with a simple click as you publish each post. Take advantage of the ease to quickly schedule and spread messages.

When preparing a post, prepare a title, short summary, then choose categories and keywords. For images, write image tags and titles for search engines and visitors.

### Title
The title, or headline, should be under 70 characters long and use two lines. The first line will include one or more keywords or phrases and publish as the title. Put the second line, or sub headline, in italics at the top of your blog post content. It supports the first headline and provides additional keywords, but is published at the top of the blog post content. If you have posted a press release, you will be familiar with this feature.

### Summary
Each blog post should have a concise summary using keywords, sometimes also called a snippet, excerpt, or meta description. If you don't include your written summary, search engines will use the first words of the post. The length limit is 155 characters to ensure is appears in its entirety in search results. Press release writers will be familiar with this feature as it is part of the process to submit a release that helps sell the piece in search results.

### Categories
Using the Category feature and keywords in blog software helps web visitors find content that interests them easily. WPbeginner.com has the best description of how to think of categories and keywords that I have read: think of categories as your table of contents and keywords as your index, as in the back of a book. As you think of the topics you expect to cover, write them down. Now consider which may be combined in one category. A doctor, for instance, might think of all the conditions that he treats and realize that joint pain and pain management should fall under a general category of "Pain." This exercise keeps the category list shorter and easier to browse.

Always choose at least one category; otherwise the blog software will default to "Uncategorized," a lame alternative that won't do justice to the time devoted to preparing each post.

## Keywords

Keywords, or tags, help visitors search on narrow topics, such as joint pain in the example above. Keywords, like categories, should be something you compile thoughtfully before you tackle any content to decide which words and phrases are the most important to your audience. Don't hesitate to create longer phrases and hundreds of them. Run them all through a service, such as Google's Keyword Planner, to capture the monthly traffic estimates for each term, then prioritize them and choose the top five that mean the most to you. Start with those and use often. Try to add more from this list as you create each new piece of content.

For each blog post, identify a focus keyword, the most important one for visitors to find your post. Use that in your title and copy. Choose and use other keywords that are on your list that would be appropriate in your post.

## Images

Images are powerful parts to blog posts, drawing interest to read the item. Photos, illustrations, videos, charts and other images help attract audience too. Image descriptions, captions, alt tags, also called alt text, and alt titles feed search engine spiders. Image tags and titles also help visually impaired and those who select text only settings understand your graphic's purpose. The alt title appears when the reader hovers over the image. While a title isn't required, each image should have the alt text to inform readers who cannot see the image.

This chapter, like all the others, serves as just a basic overview. As you begin your first efforts and get comfortable, hopefully you will be interested to learn more and get better. To help you, I provide further reading by authors I go to for answers, like those below. Enjoy the process and be patient. Your efforts will pay off.

## Further reading

To learn more about WordPress, follow WPbeginner: wpbeginner.com

"How Long Should Your Blog Post Be?" at thewritepractice.com/blog-post-length

Beginner videos for WordPress from experts: videos.wpbeginner.com This site offers terrific advice and answers.

From Yoast, provider of SEO software: What should be in your image alt tags and titles at yoast.com/image-seo-alt-tag-and-title-tag-optimization

Google: Alt tag and alt text:
https://support.google.com/webmasters/answer/114016

# Chapter 7

## Emailings and Landing Pages

### Email is not just relevant; it's essential

Emailings and landing pages are part of the foundation, or base camp, you create, which is composed of your web site, blog and social media sites where you want transactions to take place. Emailings provide the thought leadership and value that earn recognition and loyalty needed for actions by your visitors. Landing pages reaffirm and deliver what you promise.

### Emailings

Email might seem like old-school marketing today, but it remains the most important business marketing tool. For every $1 spent, email marketing generates $38 in sales. Email is still the #1 online activity[12] by 90.92% of adult Internet users and the #1 channel used by 95% of marketers. Email beats social by 40x[13] for customer acquisition. Emailings are still a primary source of sales, providing the least expensive method to nurture leads along the purchase cycle.

Successful email marketing means providing value. To stay informed, 28% of consumers subscribe to emails. When rewards are offered, a whopping 59% of moms are willing to sign up. Email coupons are important to 65% of shoppers for grocery shopping online. Consistent, thoughtful content and incentives drive fruitful returns.

Since it will likely take 7-13 touches to secure desired actions, one or more of those interactions should be through email because 1) it's cheap to deliver a message 2) the end user saw something of value by opting-in to receive email from you and 3) that value translates into better conversion than any first-time contact.

---

[12] "Is Email Marketing Dead?" https://optinmonster.com/is-email-marketing-dead-heres-what-the-statistics-show/

[13] "The New Rules of Email Marketing": https://www.campaignmonitor.com/resources/guides/email-marketing-new-rules/

## Email marketing is cheap

Your cost to send may be just a couple of cents per message. By using templates in a CAN SPAM compliant program, your time to compose, send and track is minimal. Email programs include tracking so you can instantly evaluate your response in terms of sales, leads, the number of prospects who opened a message and clicked through to the landing page.

## Subscriber relationship

By subscribing, prospects have come to know your company. You may have already provided value to them, such as a coupon, discount or white paper for signing up. Or perhaps they have already been a customer.

## Better conversion

That warm relationship of familiarity is what leads to better conversions, the process where readers click from an email, ad or web page through to make a purchase or complete some other action; better than any message emailed to a cold list of prospects would achieve. That's why it's so important to provide strong value in every message to maintain a high level of interest. A cold list might yield a 1% conversion, where 1% complete actions, while your subscribers may close at a 3% rate or better.

## Plan your email

Determine the purpose for each email, the value you will offer and list every goal you need to achieve. Here are various considerations:
1. Convey thought leadership
2. How this email fits with your 12-month editorial calendar
3. Make any announcements
   a. New personnel or partnerships
   b. Upcoming appearances, such as webinars, speeches or trade shows
   c. Upcoming publications, such as articles
   d. New products or services
   e. New freebies, such as downloads

4. Review any and all calls to action
   a. Purchase
   b. Register
   c. Download or other freebie that suits the purpose

## Components of a strong email message
1. Strong, attention-grabbing subject line
2. Personalized greetings, such as Hi Mary, increases click-through rates and conversions
3. Body copy that is short and to the point
4. Value that is highly perceived
5. CTA buttons vs. links perform 28% better; try to place above the scroll
6. Signature for a real person with URL and social icons
7. Request to forward feature
8. Company name, physical address and opt-out functionality for CAN SPAM compliance

Ask for the order. Don't be shy or annoying. Find the balance. Once complete, proofread, proofread, proofread and then have someone else proofread. Nothing is more embarrassing than a typo or misspelled name. Next, send yourself a test email to make sure all the elements look right. You might try doing it in various browsers too, in case you want to edit or reformat, so all elements display correctly.

If you use images, also provide text for those who set their email default to hide images.

A good example of a digital signature design includes a small logo, web site address, social media and other contact information. Certain industries, such as real estate, use images in email signatures more. It may seem unprofessional in others.

Make sure that your contact information is not in an image that might be hidden by a user's email preferences. You might add a link to the latest article, press release or credential.

## Catchy subject lines and headlines

Craft your email subject lines to stop readers in their tracks and keep them under 50 characters so they display completely. These are examples of formats that work to entice better open rates for professionals:

The Secrets of (blank)
What (blank) Can Teach Us about (blank)
Everything You Know about (blank) is Wrong
How (blank) Made (blank) and You Can Too

## Timing of your email blasts

However often you deliver email messages, whether monthly, weekly or daily, make it well worthwhile, or your audience may break up with you and opt-out. Commit to a regular schedule, which will likely require some planning. Generally, the best day to send an email to get optimum opens is Tuesday. Most studies suggest the best time is 10 a.m. You can set delivery times based on each time zone.

## Landing pages

The purpose of the landing page is to close the sale. Several key elements go into achieving the best conversion rate. As the Canon case study shows in Beasley Direct's white paper[14], successful changes can improve results by 50 times! Additionally, personalization delivers 50-150% better conversion.

Make visitors comfortable that they have landed in a safe environment for transactions. You want to reduce any distraction to shorten the time to seal the deal. Create short copy and graphics on the landing page like those they just left. Keep the copy short and to the point. Repeat the promises and design of the CTA page with the same style, fonts and colors. Reaffirm all promises, such as benefits, cost or free shipping

---

[14] Beasley Direct and Online Marketing's landing page white paper: https://beasleydirect.com/white_papers/capture-more-leads-with-optimized-landing-pages

offers. Consider using security badges on your site, such as Thawte or Verisign.

## CAN SPAM compliance

Email programs include formats to address the CAN SPAM law which requires the sender's physical address, contact information, opt-out functionality and privacy statement. Each emailing program provides guidance to easily set up the appropriate template and maintain a list of opt-outs, called a suppression list.

As of May 2018, those companies collecting information from European Union (EU) residents must take extra steps to gain consent, provide for access and correction of data as required by the GDPR, the General Data Protection Regulation, legislation with a penalty up to 4% of gross revenues for failure to comply. Again, software companies meet these needs related to your emailings. You will, however, set up and maintain your overall procedures and policies to serve GDPR stipulations beyond emailings.

## References and further reading

"11 reasons why your emails go into the spam box and how to make sure they don't" at https://optinmonster.com/11-reasons-why-your-emails-go-in-the-spam-box-and-how-to-make-sure-they-dont

Copyblogger's "9 Proven Headline Formulas that Sell Like Crazy" at https://copyblogger.com/proven-headline-formulas

Best days and times to send emails from CoSchedule: https://coschedule.com/blog/best-time-to-send-email

Personalization increases click-through rates by 14% and conversions by 10% from Campaign Monitor: campaignmonitor.com/blog/email-marketing/2016/01/70-email-marketing-stats-you-need-to-know

# Chapter 8

## Newsletter

### Newsletters

Used by 81% of B2B marketers[15], electronic newsletters offer your business the opportunity to establish thought leadership, gain credibility, continue a regular program of touches with your prospects and customers, expand your subscriber base and increase sales. Your customers will come to count on your perspective, insights and product catalog. Your newsletter educates, informs and helps to convert leads and sales.

Some wonder why they should bother with a newsletter when they do a blog. The difference is that a newsletter is published less frequently, usually monthly or quarterly, covers many topics and always includes self-promotional content. Blog posts just cover one topic, are generally fairly short (under 1500 words), much more frequent and don't always necessarily have a call-to-action.

As a tool, your newsletter helps to convince customers to buy, or that they made a good decision to buy from you in the past and should continue to trust and buy from you again. You can establish regular columns such as from a company owner or industry news. Use your newsletter to generate traffic back to your site, blog, products or other landing pages where you want your transactions to occur. Ask your subscribers to forward your newsletter to friends and colleagues. Include your social media icons with links for easy sharing.

Entice your web visitors to sign up for your newsletters with special offers or discounts, such as a free ebook. Create a friendly autoresponder, generated by your email program, to confirm and thank

---

[15] Content marketing usage by B2B companies:
https://contentmarketinginstitute.com/wp-content/uploads/2015/09/2016_B2B_Report_Final.pdf

them for signing up. You might take the opportunity to give them a link to a previous newsletter, other free content and/or your product catalog.

Your newsletter is also your platform to announce, recognize and remind your subscribers.

Here are a few suggestions for important topics to remember:
- New products
- Company awards
- Staff recognition
- Coupons and discounts
- First-to-know news
- Loyalty program
- Industry news
- Testimonials
- Events where team members will be, such as trade shows
- Speaking engagements
- Partnership developments

**Don't forget these basic rules:**
Consult your twelve-month editorial calendar first for upcoming events to get ideas for newsletter articles. Consider the variety of topics you will want to cover. Always think about your calls-to-action as you prepare each newsletter. Next, plan for the section to promote your company.

Use your keywords in your content; choose graphics and photos to help tell and sell. Plan to repurpose pieces or pull excerpts from other assets. For instance, use an abstract from a white paper and provide a link to download it. Create or choose images to use in blog posts and other materials in addition to the newsletters.

You'll want two versions of your newsletter, both printed and electronic. Design a template with fixed features, keeping in mind formats that can be emailed and printed. The electronic version can take advantage of hyperlinks, but you'll want to spell out URLs for the printed version.

Printed newsletters are great to use at trade shows, in sales folders, to mail with products, in sales offices and stores. Choose a nice stock to make a good impression.

Choose a strong emailing program to handle your newsletter. Sending newsletters means you will want to collect and save email addresses in a secure environment, maintain a suppression list (names of those who opted-out) and maintain compliance. The CAN SPAM law requires that you provide a way for visitors to opt-out of your emailings, your company name and your physical address.

As a good practice, observe GDPR as well as CAN SPAM compliance rules even if you only do business in the U.S. Good email software companies provide the tools to help correctly secure opt-ins and maintain databases.

Email newsletters are such an inexpensive way to deliver valuable content and stimulate sales that it makes sense to invest a little time to create a template and regularly remind your prospects and customers about your products and services in an interesting way. You may well enjoy the best return from this channel than any other avenue.

# Chapter 9
## Social Media and Other Platforms

As exciting an opportunity as social media marketing is, it's critical to remember that these activities are supporting actors to your main events: your website, blog and places where transactions occur, which might also include social media. The opportunity social media present is the ability to put unlimited messages in front of millions of prospects for free. Each little cookie crumb treat draws interested parties to your door.

**Social media and other pages that make up your web presence**
The functionality (e.g. shop and lead generation buttons) and audience as well as the kind of content you want to create (video, audio, written word) define the platforms to focus efforts that drive traffic to the pages where you want visitors to complete transactions. Certainly, you will most likely include your site and blog, but you also might consider one of the social media sites, such as Facebook, so crucial to the actions you seek that you include it in your base camp.

Now, choose ones where you will promote the content that leads to those desired actions. Expect that you will add new ones and remove others as new platforms appear and others disappear. Go ahead and list every site you would ever think to use. Then prioritize that list. Consider the rank of sites where purchases take place, such as Facebook and Instagram. Those might be more important to you; time will tell if non-transactional media will deliver more traffic that continually converts at your base camp destinations.

Next, choose just a few from the top of your list for your first efforts. There are several good reasons for this strategy, because you should:
1. Focus on getting initial results
2. Use your limited time to target traffic from the first sites you choose, and
3. Not risk burnout and get discouraged by spreading yourself too thinly

## Social media presence

First off, don't consider these sites the be-all and end-all. Sites changes over time: new ones launch and easily, I have not included ones here that might be specific to your particular business model or industry.

Once you've made choices and priorities, move on to set up each social media site. Your accounts typically require small logo icons, larger cover photos and a company description. Use this social media cheat sheet[16] to develop creative assets. Many sizes will be reused or can easily be resized.

The great thing about social media is that businesses easily get substantial traction out of a growing audience interaction. Incorporating social media into a marketing plan is a no-brainer, since business participation is free. What is also dramatically different from traditional promotion is that the nature of social media is to engage in two-way conversations with consumers. Other media: tv, radio, print, outdoor, Internet advertising, articles and press releases are all one-way pitches of informational content.

Social media give customers the opportunity to write reviews, ask questions in public and private venues, share thoughts in communities, as well as to learn from companies and other customers. Bad customer service, poorly designed products and every other business blemish are publicly visible. The experiences of individuals, both bad and good, are then shared globally.

As a marketer, you have lost control of the message. At best, you can work hard to manage the message. That's where social media can be a big benefit to you. Monitoring, participating, and engaging will improve the impression that your company makes. You can improve your

---

[16] Social Media Image Sizes: An Always-Up-to-Date Guide
https://www.rakacreative.com/blog/social-media-marketing/social-media-image-sizes-always-up-to-date/

credibility and your reputation. If something bad happens, your quick response gets noticed.

Continual one-way communication isn't and won't be successful in social media. In fact, too much pitching is not welcome. A certain amount is accepted, expected and tolerated. In moderation. To the point that there is a rule of thumb of one "pitch" or completely self-serving message to every 10-12 messages. Your customers want education and help. They want and expect coupons, discounts and rewards for their loyalty. The more attention and response you can show, the better the experience you deliver to your customer. When you work to achieve that every day, you'll reap results.

So how do you go about evaluating your progress and efforts? Even if you aren't spending ad dollars on social media (yet), your time is essentially money. Once you determine your goals, choose your platforms and post messages, you can monitor your analytics to track your progress.

## Goals
Ask yourself "What are the social media goals and expectations?" and "How do these move the overall business goals forward?" Too often company representatives jump into social media to play without a plan. Then managers looking for the results of these efforts may not see any.

It's important to start with a sense of what you want to get out of your social media experience. Taking a little time to think through the capabilities you need and want will help you build a plan and choose elements you can prioritize for implementation. It will save you time in changes you won't have to make later too.

These decisions help you with a framework of parameters based on the amount of time you can devote, your budget and the kind of experience you and your prospects, clients, colleagues and audience want. Your choices will determine how you will build out your social media presence.

**Ask these questions:**
1. Is your goal to sell more products and services?
2. Do you expect social media to be an extension of your customer service?
3. How will you engage with your prospects?
4. What level of participation are you expecting? How do you feel, for instance, about comments on your Facebook page?
5. How much time are your willing to devote to the process (per week or per month)?
6. What calls-to-action will you use?
7. Where will those actions take place?

Start by looking around at what your competition is doing. What are they doing right? What are they doing wrong? Don't just review their numbers.

If you have been out there in social media awhile, step back and take a perspective. What have you done right? What have you done wrong? Not just your numbers, but what is the quality of your reactions?

**Competitive analysis**
Don't get so wrapped up in social media numbers and forget to try to interpret, not only the numbers, but also the quality of the messages between competitors and customers. Regular retrospective social media measurement is important to success. Coupling qualitative and quantitative reviews with analysis yields a bank of actionable recommendations for improvement.

It's one thing to see how many Twitter followers or Facebook friends or blog subscribers a company has. It's quite another to see how painfully empty of content a competitors' stream of tweets may be. Or how "pitchy" all their messages are. It can be gratifying to deep dive into the quality of a clients' followers and the content of their messages. How appreciative are their customers? What are they asking for? Are they getting it?

After the quantitative and qualitative studies are in, then continue the process and watch improvement.

Competition may make some moves that can cause a reevaluation of the original set of goals. Sometimes things going on inside a company can cause that second look. New social media come onboard and things continue to change. Regular retrospective review is tantamount to success.

As long as this is low effort and low cost, the goal is to maximize the return on these efforts and move from low impact to high impact. Doing regular monthly and quarterly reviews keeps the focus on the ball. Where do you want to take it? Is it going in the right direction?

Now, what are the takeaways from what you are doing? From what your competitors are doing?

**Interact**
1. Create and use FAQs
2. Check comments; daily at a minimum
3. Be timely with responses

Becoming thoughtful of these reviews can generate exploration and creation of new, expanded tactics to continue to improve the customer experience. This can be exciting for both company and followers, as listening and interacting builds relationships further and deeper.

**Take stock of assets**
Now, take stock. Make a list of "assets." Use Content and Image Inventory templates[17]. No sense recreating the wheel when you have a ton of spokes already. Which of these do you have now? Make sure to list all the multiples of any of these. Don't let this list overwhelm you. Think of it as a starting point. You can always come back later.

---

[17] Use Content and I Templates: https://dmcenter.com/marketing-asset-management-made-easy/content-inventory and https://dmcenter.com/track-images-with-inventory-template/

| Materials | |
|---|---|
| Articles | Photos |
| Blog | Press Releases |
| Domains | Seals (security, etc.) |
| Images | Videos |
| Logos | Web site |

Do you have brand guidelines to follow that dictate the colors and fonts and other styles you should use? What copyrights, trademarks and patents do you have?

Do you have industry, trade, partner or other relationships where you share acknowledgement with their logos? Do you have all the permissions you need for those logos?

Do you have a privacy policy or notice to share with the public? Do you have other legal notices that should be shared?

**Social media accounts**

List all social media platforms in web presence:

| Social media accounts | |
|---|---|
| List all social media platforms in web presence | |
| Blog | LinkedIn (Personal) |
| Facebook (Personal) | LinkedIn Company Profile |
| Facebook Page and/or Group | Pinterest |
| Flickr | Tumblr |
| Google My Business | Twitter |
| Google Ads (access Keyword | Vimeo |
| Instagram | YouTube |

Other platforms with substantial audiences to consider include places to publish articles, such as Medium, press release sites, such as Business Wire, consumer sites such as Yelp and event sites, such as Meetup.

Even if you aren't ready to buy pay-per-click advertising on Google Ads, signing up for a free account will give you access to the Keyword Planner which is useful to choose keywords for copywriting to learn which terms are the most popular.

## Most Important sites
### LinkedIn
This site is for professionals to help establish credibility and provide a connection for business and career opportunities. At a minimum, create a Company Profile page with a powerful description and contact information. Many prospective clients and vendors will check this area while doing due diligence. Salespeople find LinkedIn an invaluable source to identify and build relationships, especially with long sales cycles. Companies create Showcase pages to increase visibility for product and service lines.

While an audience of only 250 million monthly visitors seems small, its purchase by Microsoft and focus on business professionals is significant. It's often used to research companies and individuals before accepting a meeting. Firms with B2B targets can use LinkedIn as a platform to post regularly to demonstrate thought leadership. Further, LinkedIn's SlideShare feature allows individuals to share PowerPoint presentations.

### Facebook
A force to be reckoned with, Facebook's community of over 2 billion users per month is often used by businesses to give loyal customers special treatment from their business Pages, offering coupons, previews of new products and much more. Facebook's Shop Now function makes it a potentially strong source of transactions. Its Messenger service, with 1.3 million monthly users, is great for customer service, for those who prefer that platform, and is projected to be a powerful tool for interactions. Facebook's younger audience is shifting to Instagram, while it remains a popular destination for Baby Boomers.

### YouTube
With 1.8 billion monthly users, Google's premiere video site is terrific for hosting videos that can take a lot of storage on your site. Just embed them in a post and leave the hosting to YouTube. Create a channel to build a following to your videos and those you add to your Playlists. Most YouTube accounts are limited to 15 minutes per video; however,

you can select the option to make a request to increase it. The maximum upload file size is 128 GB with maximum duration 12 hours.

## Google My Business

Important for many services, Google gives more prominence[18] to businesses that complete information for their free listing, such as hours, website, address and phone. Using your Google account to read reviews on your business allows you to respond to good and bad comments. You can also post blog posts there.

## Twitter

Take advantage of Twitter's focus on what's happening now to post timely messages. Forty percent of visitors are 18-29 and 27% are between 30 and 49 years old. Use hashtags to appeal to their audience of 321 million monthly users interested in your trade shows and subject matter. Mention others whose followers might be interested in your messages. Twitter messages, called tweets, can be up to 280 maximum characters, plus you can pack sequential tweets together or select several to create a Moment.

## Choose the next sites in importance

Certainly store-based retail would look at Yelp and Foursquare. A company in an industry that offers opportunities for visually rich presentations would look at Instagram or Pinterest; think interior design, travel, home goods and apparel, for example.

## Foursquare

Location sites are important for local retailers. Foursquare is just one that collects information about the habits of its users. Message your customers. Provide coupons; announce news.

## Instagram

With its 1 billion monthly users, Instagram is growing quickly as a visual platform for images, such as products or events. Expect that its purchase by Facebook will help drive more new traffic quickly to this image-based service. Like Facebook, it's great for longer messages than Twitter allows, for instance.

---

[18] Google: Improve your local ranking at
https://support.google.com/business/answer/7091

## Medium

A platform for long-form content, Medium boosts the most interesting articles to its 60 million monthly visitors; many are paying subscribers.

## Meetup

Find or create events to expand your network or provide education that creates interest in your business. Over 225,000 groups schedule events through Meetup.

## Mix.com

Mix recommends photos, videos and other content to its users based on their interests.

## Pinterest

A photo-sharing site with 291 million monthly users, Pinterest is also a powerful search engine. Companies might use it simply to show off awards, however, it is a terrific environment for sharing content created by your business or others. Post how-to demonstrations and finished shots of products in use. This is the place prospects post wish lists of things they want to buy and do, appealing to advertisers who seek shoppers considering lifestyle purchases where images help sell. Perfect product categories for Pinterest include fashion, food and travel.

## Quora

Answer questions on given topics to establish thought leadership as an expert. The Quora site gets 100 million visitors/month. Set preferences and questions will arrive in your inbox.

## Reddit

A site of 330 million active users, Reddit allows voting on posts and news, calendar posting, network or community creation and encourages submissions. Customer service teams review posts for great user-generated content and negative messages for their speedy response.

## SnapChat

Use SnapChat to post pictures and 10-second videos to its 301 million (mostly teenage) active users per month to promote coupons, giveaways, events, demonstrations and cross-promotion to other sites.

**SoundCloud**
Store podcasts where 175 million people listen each month. Promote and share from your sites.
**Tumblr**
Another network of users who have shared over 171 billion posts of text, photos and video.
**Vimeo**
This is another important site (170 million visitors/month) which is used for hosting and sharing videos.
**Yelp**
This is another key site (145 million visitors/month) for local businesses where businesses can capture the interest of prospects as they are searching for services in their category. This site also allows reviews, which businesses should monitor and respond to regularly.

**Promotion**
If you haven't already, create an editorial calendar by listing upcoming events for your company, industry or personnel. A retail store would plot annual sales, holidays and local activities.
**Social media messaging**

**Messaging workflow**
**Upon project start-up and annually thereafter:**
1. Set up messaging spreadsheets

**Monthly:**
2. Consult editorial calendar, review CTAs for lead generation or transactions
3. Collect ideas, links and write messages
4. Format and schedule
5. Pull reports and analyze

**Report Set-up**

1. At the beginning of the year and for each project, I set up a spreadsheet for each social media channel with a tab for each month.

The header row has a column for the date the message is posted, another for the message and a third for a link that the message promotes.

2. Next, I add tabs for Keywords, FAQs, Hashtags, Affiliate Links, Research and Evergreen, or frequently used, messages. I prioritize keywords for the site and topics. The FAQs tab holds answers to questions with frequently used responses. Affiliate links are unique links, specific to a product or service, that give monetary credit to the referring site for performance by its visitors. Research includes links to industry and other important sites that are frequently mentioned in messages. The Evergreen tab includes links and customized shortened links to a website home or landing pages, for instance.

3. I maintain these spreadsheets to easily find previous messages and links later. This is helpful when trying to track messages down again for reuse, when links become broken or for marketing accountability in the event of client, legal and other oversight.

4. Review the messaging needs of the editorial calendar each month. Time messages to precede and coincide with events, such as trade shows or product launches.

5. Use an RSS feed reader to collect respected newsletters and choose articles from peers and industry to add to your promotional and educational posts to share with your audience.

6. Write and format messages, such as shortening links for promotion. Make sure to proofread to avoid embarrassment.

7. I save time by scheduling a month's worth of messages at a time. Then as news impacts business, I add messages, repost and interact on the fly.

8. Monitor competitor sites for opportunities to respond intelligently and helpfully.
9. Pull statistics from Google Analytics and each of the social media platforms monthly. Look at reviews, mentions and direct messages to evaluate the quality of interactions and what might be done differently to improve business and responses. Transaction statistics will include cost-per-click, cost-per-impression and cost-per-sale for analysis.

## Tools
Briefly, since you'll find more in the Marketing Tools chapter, find key tools to track (Google analytics account and Cyfe), schedule posts (Hootsuite) and shorten URLs (Bit.ly).

## Action items
Retailers: Join Google Local Business, get a free listing and claim your business at (You will need a Gmail account).

## Experts to follow
To learn more about Facebook, follow Mari Smith's blog
https://www.marismith.com/mari-smith-blog

To learn more about WordPress, follow WPbeginner.com

# Chapter 10
## Back-end Management: Accepting Payments

I refer to this next group of services as back-end operations. If you think of product development as the front of the house, then shipping, fulfillment, customer service and credit card processing along with accounting, make up the back. If this area isn't pertinent or of interest, move on to Chapter 13, Retail Strategy. My feelings won't be hurt.

It's easy for small businesses, needing to accept credit cards, to make expensive mistakes when choosing a payment processor because the fine print of the Terms and Conditions is difficult to read and understand. Most new companies are eager to get set up quickly and fail to recognize that these agreements are negotiable. Contracts allow processors to control the flow of funds from transactions which affect the ability to conduct business. Startups also often don't realize these contracts stipulate rules that merchants must follow to retain the privilege to accept credit cards.

The agreement between merchant and processor generally favors the processor, who tries to minimize their risk of advancing funds from transactions while waiting for payments from the customer's (issuing) bank. One area of concern, for instance, is the likelihood that unsatisfied customers will contact their bank to refuse payment, thus incurring a chargeback to the merchant's account. The greater the number of chargebacks, the more penalties and fees to the merchant, which may ultimately place the account in jeopardy.

The contract will detail terms. If you are a startup, read yours carefully and ask questions. Determine what the delay will be to have access to funds. It may require a three-year agreement; you may prefer a month-to-month. Merchants may prefer their bank for convenience; however, their bank is likely to charge more than other providers, making it worthwhile to shop a few different companies. An agreement may require exclusivity, precluding the ability to shop around.

Choices will include types of equipment for retail outlets for in-person transactions which merchants may rent or purchase.

## Negotiating credit card processing costs

Previous processing statements for those renegotiating services are critical for prospective processors to determine not only what previous rates were, but also the level of risk through types of transactions, numbers of chargebacks which speak to how a merchant handles returns.

## Rates

The base rate charged to a merchant for card processing is called a discount rate, which includes the cost from the association, such as MasterCard or Visa, plus a cost from the processor. A processor offers a rate based on the amount of risk it anticipates. Their underwriting staff evaluates the types of transactions, the merchants' industry, where transactions will be conducted and considers previous history. For instance, because a retailer swiping a card in their store is less likely to receive a fraudulent purchase, customer online purchases generally require a higher card-not-present charge.

## Fees

While some processors offer a basic flat rate, others require an additional per transaction fee. They may require other fees, such as an annual compliance fee for services to help merchants respond to requirements by the Payment Card Industry (PCI). For most companies, compliance includes a self-assessment survey and quarterly test to scan devices involved in transactions for privacy and security.

## Reserve

The merchant agreement generally allows processors the ability to hold back funds, depending upon anticipated risk. This deposit may increase as circumstances change. For instance, merchants who suffer data breaches may experience an increase in withheld funds, called the reserve. Merchants with an increasing number of returns or fraudulent transactions may also be subject to increases.

## Merchant responsibilities

The ability to accept credit and debit payments is a privilege. This financial partnership requires details such as loans and comes with responsibilities to maintain the privilege.

1. Manage customer service and reduce chargebacks
   a. Name on credit card statements with toll-free number

Select a name to show up on consumers' card statements so they will know immediately what that purchase was for and include a toll-free number directly going to customer service on the same line.

   b. Satisfy customers quickly

Consumer happiness is the #1 concern of the card associations (MasterCard, Visa, Discover, American Express). Set up and follow procedures to respond expeditiously to customer issues so they don't turn to their card company for a chargeback.

2. Working to keep good relationship with processors

Demonstrate best efforts to secure customer data. Learn from processing staff, encourage feedback and keep an ongoing discussion about how to avoid fraud.

3. Make every effort to reduce fraud
   a. Wi-fi environment and firewall

Become familiar with your services; learn how your IT team sets up and maintains systems.

   b. Employee rules/training for handling physical and electronic data

Your staff, partners and vendors play a key part in keeping your customer data and your business safe. Diagram how data is handled by each player as it comes into your organization, through it and is finally destroyed.

   c. PCI compliance

Take your annual survey with your team. Conduct scanning and remediation steps as needed. Repeat with any substantial change to equipment or systems.

**Further reading**
First Data's Payments 101 primer:
https://firstdata.com/downloads/thought-leadership/payments101wp.pdf

What You Need to Know about Credit Card Processing:
https://boss.blogs.nytimes.com/2013/03/25/what-you-need-to-know-about-credit-card-processing

Payment Processing Primers:
Merchant Maverick Beginner's Guide
https://merchantmaverick.com/beginners-guide-payment-processing-ebook
JBD Consulting http://jbdconsulting.us/wp-content/uploads/2015/03/JBD-Consulting-Payment-processing-primer.pdf

Visa Interchange Rates 2019:
https://usa.visa.com/dam/VCOM/download/merchants/visa-usa-interchange-reimbursement-fees.pdf

The Complete Guide to Credit Card Processing from Merchant Maverick: https://merchantmaverick.com/the-complete-guide-to-credit-card-processing-rates-and-fees

# Chapter 11
## Back-end Management: Telemarketing

When you think of telemarketing, you may not realize the large number of options or the breadth of what telemarketing services can do for your business. Companies conduct customer service by taking inbound calls, handling live chat on web sites, responding to web and email requests to call outbound, implementing Interactive Voice Response (IVR) recordings to accept inbound or execute outbound calls, gather information and route calls (such as prescription readiness notifications from drugstores) to live operators and other personnel.

Providing excellent customer service should be top of every company's priorities because those relationships lead to further sales, increased average orders, referrals and great reviews. However, other interactions can be fruitful. Calling customers to conduct a satisfaction or preference survey or make a special offer often yields further sales.

As I've mentioned earlier, marketers have learned that customers can remain engaged during a call where up to five additional products and services, called upsells, are offered, before customer fatigue risks the loss of the sale. Results are best when the upsells are closely related to the original item.

Live operators are not an inexpensive proposition, so plan the process in great detail. Skilled teams, however, often do a wonderful job of overcoming objections and increasing the average sale. Firms often combine some automation to reduce call time, for instance, to collect some initial information or even complete an entire order.

If you have never written a telemarketing script before, a telemarketer will provide scripting help. A small team is generally educated about the script and then tests it to a small group of customers. Clients share in the development and training. The better the call team understands the offer, the better a job they will do, especially since they will take calls for many other clients at the same time. Clients are invited to listen in. After testing, changes might be implemented for further testing, followed by rollout into the full campaign. Tweaks continue with experience and as new products or services are added or modified.

Preparation includes using an extensive set of Frequently Asked Questions (FAQs) for call center staff to consult during training and thereafter with customers. Decisions should be made to offer downsells, where customers can buy fewer products at lower prices, and incentives with proper language for continuity or autoship, where customers agree to receive regular shipments ongoing in the future. Operators should be empowered with options to help facilitate and appease customers.

## Toll-free numbers

Choosing a vanity number, one whose numbers also spell a name or words to increase memorability (such as 1-800-Flowers), can be especially helpful in campaigns that will air extensively on radio. Direct response campaigns using toll-free numbers need a different phone number airing on TV stations separated by at least 500 miles so responses can be attributed correctly to each individual short TV spot or longer infomercial.

Many firms will charge by the minute. Some offer a pay-per-call option; make sure not to confuse it with pay-for-performance. Pay-per-call activities do not guarantee customer response.

## Legal restrictions

We have all had frustrating experiences with live and recorded telemarketers, so it should be no surprise that there are a number of laws such as the FTC's Telemarketing Sales Rule[19], the Do-Not-Call Implementation Act[20] and the FCC's Telephone Consumer Protection

---

[19] FTC's Telemarketing Sales Rule: https://ftc.gov/tips-advice/business-center/guidance/complying-telemarketing-sales-rule
[20] Do-Not-Call Implementation Act: https://en.wikipedia.org/wiki/National_Do_Not_Call_Registry

Act[21]. As of this writing, the FCC voted to make it easier for telecom providers to block unsolicited recorded calls, or robocalls.

The Direct Marketing Association (DMA), now folded into the Association of National Advertisers, created the 10 Steps to Making a Sale under the FTC's Telemarketing Rule[22]. The rules are obviously different from country to country.

Just one more reason why hiring an experienced service to craft a telemarketing script, train and supervise staff and analyze reports is so critical to success.

### Further reading
Jeff Glickman, a leader in the direct marketing field, wrote a wonderfully detailed report that gives an education to give great ideas for telemarketing uses in campaigns. Find it at bit.ly/DRTVSecrets.

---

[21] FCC's Telephone Consumer Protection Act:
https://en.wikipedia.org/wiki/Telephone_Consumer_Protection_Act_of_1991
[22] "10 Steps to Making a Sales under the FTC's Telemarketing Rule":
https://thedma.org/resources/compliance-resources/ftc-telemarketing-sales-rule

# Chapter 12
## Back-end Management: Shipping & Fulfillment

How companies ship products can make a big impression on customers. Make it a good one. It also seriously impacts your company's expenses. Make it a small one. Spend a little time to determine the best choices.

Considerations include labelling, packaging, costs to ship, pick, pack and store inventory. The ability to access accurate reports instantly regarding shipping and inventory are critical to management. Take into account costs for insurance and monthly minimums. Think about needs for security, climate controls, inventory turnover, sizes of products, shipping options (UPS, USPO, FedEx, 1-day, 5-7 day, etc.), customer service and how you would like returns handled. Determine the integration options between your ecommerce site and shipping facility. Decide whether you'll handle customer service in-house or pay a fulfillment house.

### Labelling
Make sure your customers will know immediately that the product being delivered is what they ordered from you. Reduce returns with clearly marked packages and return labels. Amazon is a good role model for the unmistakable name and smiling logo. Include return labels or provide an easy way to get them.

### Packaging
Think of ways you can delight your customers with simple packaging techniques. Carefully choose boxes because size and shape matter when it comes to shipping costs. Stuffers provide the opportunity for additional sales and customer satisfaction. You might include a catalog, reorder form, or product sample with a return label. Ask for reviews and referrals. Provide an easy way and/or discount for customers to sign up for recurring automatic shipments. Facilitating easy returns reduces chargebacks and unhappy customers who might let the world know on social media.

## Shipping

Choose the shipping options you want to make available to your customers: overnight, two-day, and/or standard shipping. Decide whether you will pass through the costs to customers or mark up the services. If you offer free shipping, determine whether there will be a threshold to spend a certain amount to qualify.

## Other choices

Find out how your shipping/fulfillment company candidates provide security, especially if you have high-value items. Review options for foods or cosmetics you may carry, such as climate controls. Ask whether customer service teams are available to take and make calls; learn what those services cost. Generally, vendors use a set of FAQs with procedures to escalate difficult calls to you, such as technical and reputation management issues.

## Amazon

The big gorilla in the room, Amazon, may be the best bet for many companies. While the costs are slightly more per shipment with a delay in funds, the ease to let Amazon collect payment, ship, handle customer service and returns may be worth it. The ability to take advantage of speedy Amazon Prime shipping makes customers happy; the average 10% increase in volume merchants realize makes them happy too. Use the link in Further Reading to determine if Amazon is right for you.

## Further reading

Shopify's Shipping and Fulfillment 101 includes photos of Trunk Club's memorable packaging and a description of GameKlip Candy as an added unpacking surprise:
https://cdn.shopify.com/s/files/1/0070/7032/files/shippingGuide_BLO G.pdf

Educational comparison of services:
https://fitsmallbusiness.com/order-fulfillment-services

Get matched to a fulfillment service. Take a survey of needs: http://thebest3plcompanies.com/lead_widgets/insightquote

Calculate whether Amazon's shipping is right for you: https://sellercentral.amazon.com/hz/fba/profitabilitycalculator/index?lang=en_US

How to Select the Best Fulfillment Services Company for your Business: https://fulfillmentcompanies.net/how-to-select-the-best-fulfillment-services-company-for-your-business

# Chapter 13

## Retail distribution

Retail distribution takes strategy to balance pricing and offer configurations between ecommerce, brick and mortar stores and Amazon.

### Brick and mortar retail stores

When seeking retail distribution, only 2% of applicants get accepted, so get your ducks in a row. Get the product in its best version of itself. Document the process to expand manufacturing exponentially. Calculate costs carefully and forecast ways to reduce costs even more. Prepare a concise, thorough presentation and complete applications thoughtfully.

Remember that retailers will always ask for your marketing and media plans to support sales. If you plan to sell direct-to-consumer prior to a retail rollout, retailers may ask to have the product available to them within six months of launch. They also do not want to see consumer direct campaigns that compete or defeat retail sales, so coordinate pricing and offer configuration carefully.

### Retail considerations: costs and time
1.  Low wholesale price
Big retailers drive hard bargains; know your best price.
2.  Long approval process
Realize that the process may take months, be patient, positive and plan accordingly.
3.  Meeting supplier requirements
Getting DUNS numbers, liability insurance, UPC codes and more may be overwhelming.
4.  Pricing at retail vs. online vs. Amazon
Carefully review product pricing across sales channels and over time to avoid potholes that cripple future sales. You can't sustain and grow a

business that isn't profitable. Fight to sock away money for unforeseen expenses as well as develop new products and services.

Don't let surprise expenses in legal, accounting or inventory sidetrack your ability to move forward with retail distribution. Plan carefully.

Another road to retail may be to start with local and regional retailers first. A strong track record helps to make the case in a very competitive environment for the attention and shelf space of a retailer. Find additional prospects with a little research at your local library or purchase a list of retail buyers for as little as $200 from Chain Store Guide[23] or Salesman's Guide[24].

## Amazon

Amazon certainly makes it easy for manufacturers to sell directly from their platform. Think of it: Amazon collects the credit card information, ships product and can handle customer service. It costs a little bit more to have them do it all. However, building the infrastructure may be well worth it.

The biggest advantages to selling on Amazon include 1) the high visibility (80% of customers do research on Amazon), 2) Prime shipping boost sales by 10% on average, and 3) good reviews are an important plus to every brand.

Since you know your products better than Amazon does, you may prefer to handle customer questions directly. You may prefer to ship directly in order to put promotional material that Amazon might not approve. Repackaging your own returns will likely look more professional. At the end of the day, you will own your relationship with customers where you cannot when Amazon does the work.

---

[23] Chain Store Guide: https://chainstoreguide.com
[24] The Salesman's Guide: http://www.retailsalesconnect.com/

Amazon has a lot of rules that you must follow or risk suspension. That's why I recommend starting with an Amazon consultant to learn the ropes. Big Commerce published The Definitive Guide to Selling on Amazon (see Further Reading at the end of the chapter) which will teach you enough to know that you need help — at least initially. Running out of inventory, too many returns or bad reviews may all be cause for termination. Contact me for a referral to an expert.

Going up on Amazon requires a plan, not just for delivering inventory, messaging customers and handling returns, but also for pricing. Amazon does not want to be undersold, so have higher prices on your own site and make sure partners never undersell your price on Amazon. You may need to reconfigure your offers on your site.

## Home shopping: QVC

Don't kid yourself that Shark Tank's Lori Grenier has a lock on QVC. See below for the link to apply to be a vendor on QVC. It might take you a little longer than Lori, but if the fit is right, you can do it.

Again, you'll need to do some planning. QVC requires a minimum of units to be at their fulfillment center before they promote a product, which will mean an investment and shipping of some 3000 products. Also, it's preferable to have your own pitchperson to share the promotion on stage with QVC's personality and even better if the person has a history of doing so on QVC.

See Further Reading for a list of U.S. shopping channels.

## Further reading

Purchase lists of contact information for buyers:
The Chain Store Guide: https://chainstoreguide.com
The Salesman's Guide: http://www.retailsalesconnect.com

How to Sell to Walmart and Other Big Box Stores: https://www.thebalancesmb.com/how-to-sell-to-walmart-and-other-big-box-retailers-2948331

Submitting products to a big box store
Walmart: https://corporate.walmart.com/suppliers
Target: https://corporate.target.com/about/products-services/suppliers
Costco: https://www.costco.com/vendor-inquiries.html
Home Depot: https://homedepotlink.homedepot.com/en-us/becomesupplier/Pages/default.aspx

Amazon: The Definitive Guide:
https://www.bigcommerce.com/blog/selling-on-amazon

13 Ways to Get Kicked Off Amazon:
http://go.channeladvisor.com/rs/channeladvisor/images/us-wp-13-ways-to-get-kicked-off-amazon%20(1).pdf?link=button

List of U.S. TV shopping channels:
https://en.wikipedia.org/wiki/List_of_United_States_pay_television_channels#Shopping

QVC application: https://www.qvchsnproductpitch.com

# Chapter 14

## International

Before you launch into international or cross-border ecommerce, you'll want to do some planning. I can't begin to cover everything you need to know for your particular set of circumstances, but I'll give you a lot to chew on as well as some places and people to go to for help. Here's a list of areas for consideration and decisions:

- Countries
- Trademarks and patents
- Currencies
- Regulations
- Tariffs
- Logistics
- Pricing
- Import/export code
- Distribution
- Operations
- Creative adaption

### Countries

Your strategy may be to start with English-speaking countries first, or you may want to do add Canada and Mexico. Whichever countries you add, you will need to consider translation of your website and materials, the culture and available methods of distribution as well as regulation of your product and industry. In South Korea, for instance, export is done through consolidators who coordinate container shipments.

### Trademarks and patents

U.S. patents and intellectual property rights are not protected elsewhere, so you'll want to secure patents in other countries and get the advice of good counsel.

### Regulations

Countries may not accept certain products, such as sport drinks, soap or nutraceuticals. Any product with chemicals might need to be made in Europe and Asia to compete globally.

### Tariffs

Tariffs may be lower depending upon the category you choose for your product. For instance, defining goods as fashion jewelry versus other jewelry categories cuts costs when marketing in Asia.

### Pricing

Be careful to price in currencies. A U.K. retailer only put EU prices on products sold to U.S. consumers. That was OK when the two currencies were on par, but once that changed, they had to adjust.

### Import/export code

Many countries stipulate codes for product and electricity standards, certifications, packing and consumer relations.

### Distribution

Sometimes the best way to enter the international market is to find distribution networks, such as TV or online shopping channels. That way you just ship to one location and get the exposure of a large marketplace platform. Amazon, Alibaba and eBay are examples.

Perhaps licensing or joint ventures would work well.

Finally, direct selling to consumers may prove worthwhile and certainly can be combined with other efforts.

### Operations

Offering products to other countries will impact every department and aspect of your business. You'll need to determine return policies that comply with each country's rules. For instance, it may cost more to have a product returned than to have a consumer just keep it. Those costs certainly must be taken into consideration when pricing.

You'll need to determine the language of policies to be compliant, for instance, with the EU's GDPR consumer privacy rule. Then you must post those policies publicly on your website. Speaking of language, you'll need to translate your site and landing pages.

Your choice of services may change to find those that accommodate international needs. Tax software, such as Avalara's may do the trick.

## Creative adaptation

What is funny in the U.S. may be inscrutable in Asia, so every campaign must be built with the behavior of the target, their culture and language to be successful. Certainly, size and format adjustments must be made for each genre.

## Resources

List of international shopping channels:
https://blog.linnworks.com/complete-list-of-online-marketplaces

Protect your online brand overseas:
https://www.export.gov/article?id=Protect-Your-Online-Brand

Further consideration re: distribution approaches to exporting:
https://www.export.gov/article?id=Approaches-to-Exporting

U.S. export free educational series on exporting:
https://www.export.gov/article?id=Export-Education

Contact a trade specialist near you: https://2016.export.gov/eac

China: https://china.usembassy-china.org.cn/business/getting-started-china

# Chapter 15

## Policies & Procedures

As you grow your company, hire employees, work with partners, hire vendors, participate in trade associations, create products and service consumers, you will create a series of policies and procedures. A set of these documents increases the value and attractiveness of a startup seeking funding or a company with an exit strategy to sell all or part of itself. It may include standard agreements, contracts, disclosures, disclaimers and more.

Write and implement procedures in conjunction with legal counsel to best protect business interests. Consider record-keeping, agreements, operational processes, human resources, accounting, sales and marketing, disaster recovery, password-keeping, acceptable use of Internet, network, email and communications. Records include patents, copyrights, trademarks. Standard contract forms include non-disclosure as well as employee and partner agreements.

Laws and rules affecting ecommerce businesses regulate telemarketing, emailings, credit card processing, privacy, security, and more. Local, state, federal and international authorities each weigh in. The FTC, for instance, dictates rules regarding false claims and blogger notification of fees for reviews that require public disclosure statements. Additionally, partners, such as Amazon, require that disclaimers and disclosures of affiliates be posted on sites.

Most ecommerce sites post Terms of Service, which may include definitions, accountability, opt-out policies, payment details, dispute resolution details and the like. Companies must post privacy notices on their websites with statements of web visitor data collected and how it is used and/or shared.

Teams that create and supervise policies and procedures include human resources, IT, marketing, customer service, administration and management. Managers create and enforce internal privacy policies within companies which spell out how employees, partners and vendors must handle data to be compliant with HIPAA and other laws.

These are just some areas to cover internally and with counsel. Industry-specific rules, such as for the health care organizations, certainly must be addressed as well.

## A little about privacy and security

Protection of consumer privacy is growing in importance and in penalties for failure to secure. When the FTC first began to enforce privacy legislation, it often did not penalize companies financially. Today, fines continue to escalate as companies are expected to be aware of rules that affect their businesses. All 50 states have data breach laws and the number of rules affecting each organization depends upon what data is collected, where they are located, where they do business and more.

Most businesses today that accept credit cards are aware of the Payment Card Industry's (PCI) standard of rules[25] to follow to protect consumer information. The PCI standard generally requires, at minimum, an annual survey by companies to demonstrate compliance. Many companies go further to conduct quarterly scans of their network systems.

Credit card information is just some of the data that businesses collect that must be protected. Health care providers and their business associates, for instance, must protect patient information under national HIPAA (Health Insurance Portability and Accountability) regulations. Further laws, both federal and state protect and enforce information collected about children, seniors and consumers.

Each company should determine which fields of information are collected, transmitted and stored by their organization, which laws, regulations and rules affect their business or hire a legal or consulting

---

[25] PCI Standard: https://www.pcisecuritystandards.org

firm to aid them. It's a good idea to diagram all information from the time it comes in an organization, how it circulates internally, possibly externally and returned, how it is stored and when and how it is destroyed.

Ecommerce businesses have the additional complication of the variety of international standards, many stiffer than those in the U.S. The European Union's General Data Protection Regulation (GDPR) rule took effect in May of 2018 and while most companies doing business regularly have put procedures in place, many have not. The penalty for non-compliance may be as high as 4% of worldwide turnover (read: gross revenue), so it's smart to prepare systems and staff, then monitor regularly.

Examples of data to be protected may include name, physical address, email address, phone, health information, Social Security and drivers' license numbers, birthdates, religion, ethnicity and more, including employee and partner information as well as customers.

**Further reading**
Get a GDPR Readiness Assessment for free: https://www.veritas.com/form/whitepaper/evaluate-your-gdpr-readiness

# Phase II
## Get Set! Content

Posting a good amount of content helps to attract traffic. The more content, the more keywords, the more links, the more likely you'll get more traffic. However, frequency alone isn't enough. Content needs to be relevant. Google's search engine rewards lots of fresh content that causes web visitors to linger with higher results on search pages.

What's a good amount? At a minimum, I recommend starting a new blog, podcast or other channel with at least five posts to put up initially. For a site, the amount of copy will be directly related to the number and complexity of products, services and topics. A site for a simple impulse item may only need a few pages.

In general, once you commit to a platform, keep the content coming in a steady stream. That's the best way to determine its effectiveness. Give each platform enough love by posting, engaging and sharing over a period of at least a few months before evaluating conclusively.

**Key takeaway**
Volume, customer focus, quality and consistent posting win the day to continually attract worthwhile prospects.

# Chapter 16

## Content Overview

### Message with purpose

Now that you've established your goals, calls-to-action (CTAs), available budget and your base camp, you can turn your attention to content creation. Focus on what you want to achieve. So many marketers miss opportunities by failing to implement a strategy. Messages often go into the ether and businesses wonder why they get no orders.

Your key sites and pages where you want visitors to complete their actions, including those social media platforms where you plan transactions, form your web presence, or what I call your base camp. Your components may change over time; whatever your base camp looks like, prepare all your messaging to drive visitors to your base camp collection.

### Appealing fresh + frequent content = increased traffic plus higher search rankings

Content is king because of its appeal to an audience, and therefore, to search engines. Posting good content regularly with some frequency also helps your site get noticed by search engines. Every word published about your company can help you achieve your goals. That's why it's important to manage your entire program of content development and distribution well.

### Better yet: focused content = measurable results

Your analytics of page views for posts, releases, videos and other content will help determine what topics get the most traffic to guide future editorial choices. The "spray and pray" philosophy by blasting untargeted emails, wastes time and energy. Set up and monitor Google Analytics (see Exercise at end of chapter) to see where your visitors are spending the most time on your site. Target your audience by writing and delivering messages to drive prospects to complete your chosen actions. Your continual refinement of content and process to expedite conversion then yields improved ROI.

## It's not about you anymore

Traditional advertising, such as print, radio, tv and outdoor, broadcast messages in a shotgun approach that gets no engagement with your prospects. Marketing is no longer a one-way street where you control the message with your one voice. Today, your customers and partners expand the reach of your company and messaging. Reviews, for instance, are an example of content your customers control. How you respond to comments and reviews is important to your reputation. You want to respond quickly to address issues and thank these potential evangelists. Keep in mind that your competitors may well be reaching out to your prospects and customers. Look at the messages that your competitors, their customers and prospects publish. Take advantage of opportunities to develop a helpful relationship with your competitors' prospects as well as your own.

## What it takes to convert

Getting an audience to complete an action isn't so easy because it's not about you and your one-sided messages anymore. These days, search, discovery, research, comparison, decision, peer review and trust play parts in awareness, consideration and purchase activities.

Types of content in your scope:

- What you create and share
- What your customers create and share
- What you create with partners and customers –and share
- What you pay for –and yes, share
- What you curate from like-minded others that resonate with your ideas

Gini Dietrich of Spin Sucks came up with the PESO model to help explain newer concepts of Paid, Earned, Shared and Owned content.

## Total control

An organization creates collateral, press releases, articles, ads, webinars, videos, a web site, newsletter and blog to communicate messages totally under their control. They extend this Owned content to approved Paid content, such as incentivized brand ambassadors and company-developed content shared by affiliates.

A company may also jointly create content with partners, vendors and industry colleagues that is also approved, and so is considered under the company's control as a participant. This content may be published for free or as an ad and may appear in publications as well as the web sites of partners, vendors or industry colleagues.

Content of other like-minded creators shared by the company is generally free and completely controlled.

### Less control

Content with less control includes media interviews by print, broadcast and podcast hosts and may be free or paid ads. Paid reviews and referrals, handled within the scope of the FTC disclosure rule, are also not completely controlled by the organization.

Review this checklist when you create content:
1) Consider the *purpose(s)* to fulfill
2) Review the *goal(s)* apply
3) Choose the *CTA(s)* that fit
4) Determine the *target audience(s)*
5) Decide which base camp *destination(s)* to promote
6) Note the appropriate *length(s)* for each base camp site
7) Keep it simple (KISS)
   a) Tell 'em what will tell them
   b) Tell 'em
   c) Tell 'em what you told them

### No control

Earned media, however, which includes comments, reviews and referrals, may swing negatively or positively. Therefore, strict monitoring is called for to respond quickly to resolve customer issues and create delighted reviews. This process of reputation management is critical in the social media age when any delay can create a landslide of ill will. Positive user-generated content (UGC) is a godsend to marketers to collate testimonial social proof. With permission, the best messages should be shared by the owner.

Touches with your audience may occur via web search, landing on a page of your site or blog, social, event or peer interaction, email or digital marketing methods. Be patient. It can easily take upwards of 7-13 touches to get a consumer to respond.

Frequent, compelling subject matter helps to drive prospects to take actions. Shepherd your audience's attention to purpose, choice of target audience, calls-to-action, tone of voice, scheduling, distribution, reputation and budget management.

## Purpose
The intent of your message and placement will drive other decisions. For instance, educational materials must be more objective than self-promotional pieces. Readers presume collateral materials will boast about company strengths, but when it comes to white papers, they expect serious, objective presentations.

## Target audience
A review of your market and reader profile for each specific placement will guide your target audience(s) which, in turn, will induce the voice for each message. A white paper might be targeted at CXO level executives rather than support staff, so the writing would be professional and tailored to be receptive to that audience. Your messages on Twitter, called micro-messages, can be more informal.

## Call-to-action
Decide what action(s) you want your audience to take with each marketing piece. Whatever the transaction, registration or download, you'll make the best use of your efforts and achieve the best ROI to craft the shortest, smoothest transition to your desired result.

## Tone of voice

Each channel's profile, coupled with your corporate approach, whether professional and authoritative or quirky and fun, will dictate writing style. A press release, for instance, must be objective and written in third person, while a blog post is typically less formal, subjective and may tell a story. Here's a good article about tone of voice[26].

## Scheduling and distribution

Most messages can be scheduled to be posted ahead of time, easing time management. Take advantage of specific audiences in Facebook or LinkedIn groups for public distribution of your message. Press releases are another opportunity to choose geographical, trade industry and other circulation.

## Reputation

While you no longer have complete control over messages about your firm, you can create procedures to help avoid PR nightmares. Website visitors can make or break a company's reputation. That's why monitoring and timely response is so critical. Your site, blog and social media that allow comments must be assigned to staff for constant review of every mention. Answer quickly and appropriately. These answers have the potential to turn unhappy customers into advocates and defuse potentially viral complaints.

Social media also present new opportunities for advertisers to enjoy the praises of customers and reviewers. Everything from liking a page to favoring of a message, rave review or comment all accumulate impressions that linger a long time.

## Budget

Much of the content that is produced can be done with a little time. Many services to post and schedule offer a free basic subscription. Costs can be minor, such as a few hundred dollars, to use one of the better

---

[26] Smashing Magazine: https://www.smashingmagazine.com/2012/08/finding-tone-voice

press release services. Monitoring and creative services require RFP estimates. Paid advertising and sponsored content certainly take analysis for potential audience size and ROI to make good choices that yield close budget approximations for testing and rollout.

The fascinating Conversation Prism graphic[27] depicts the myriad of content and considerations for purpose, tone of voice, authorship, credibility and paid vs. free content, whether the content is aimed at retailers and scheduling capabilities.

**Summary**
1. Fresh, frequent content boosts search rankings in results
2. Focus content on your purpose, goals and CTAs
3. Plan and create compelling content frequently and consistently
4. When customers, prospects and partners comment, reply quickly and thoughtfully

**Exercise**
If you haven't yet, install Google Analytics on your site: https://support.google.com/analytics/answer/1008015?hl=en

In the next chapters, we'll look at content planning and the types of content you can create.

---

[27] ConversationPrism.com

# Chapter 17

## Content Planning

### Create your editorial calendar

### Why you need an editorial calendar
Better planning, across the scope of your organization's plans over the next 12-18 months, ensures adequate preparation to: 1) effectively organize authors and 2) meet deadlines for important marketing opportunities. Blocking out critical dates helps stakeholders visualize commitments and establish a sequence of activities to successfully support and promote thought leadership, products and services while making the most of resources and time.

### What to consider
List events over the coming months that have an impact on your company. Here's a list of editorial consideration possibilities for some ideas.

| Editorial Considerations |
|---|
| • Trade shows |
| • New product or service introductions |
| • Webinar or podcast events |
| • Seasonal sales or celebrations |
| • Awards |
| • Milestones |
| • New personnel and staff changes |
| • Publications |
|    o White papers |
|    o eBooks |
|    o Infographics |
|    o Articles |

Next, consider the goals of those events as you think about the various channels available to promote those activities.

New employees, products and services might all require press releases. Separately, your marketing plan for a new product release may include a white paper as well as prominence in your newsletter and emailings, along with creation of sales sheets, brochures and other collateral, presentations, videos and webinars.

## Initial planning

Collectively, an initial planning session should cover marketing goals, events, initiatives related to products and services. Then proceed to determine how to market these initiatives. The Editorial Calendar template[28] illustrates how it might support goals.

The first worksheet for Events lays out company activities and goals. The second tab, Content, details the supporting promotional elements, such as emailings, newsletters and articles. Finally, the third tab, Assignments, helps to meet deadlines by various contributors along with hashtags and keywords pertinent to events and campaigns as well as preferred and selected image notes.

Editorial Calendar – Events Tab – 12-month Plan

### Editorial Calendar Template - Events

| January | February | March | April | May | June | July | August | September | October | November | December |
|---|---|---|---|---|---|---|---|---|---|---|---|
| New Year's resolutions | New product introduction | Personnel announcement | Trade show | White paper | Update announcement | Article | White paper | Trade show | Article | White paper | Holiday |
| Article | White paper | | Co-author article announcement | | | | Industry legislation | | | | |
| | | | Article | | | | | | | | |

In the example shown, two trade shows are blocked out with an illustration of how one might be promoted with an emailing prior to the show, just before the show and post-show to follow up with potential leads. Your newsletter would carry stories and announcements prior to and/or after the shows.

Editorial Calendar – Content Tab – 12-month Plan

### Editorial Calendar Template - Content

| Month | January | February | March | April | May | June | July | August | September | October | November | December |
|---|---|---|---|---|---|---|---|---|---|---|---|---|
| | Newsletter 1 | Newsletter 2 | Newsletter 3 | Newsletter 4 | Newsletter 5 | Newsletter 6 | Newsletter 7 | Newsletter 8 | Newsletter 9 | Newsletter 10 | Newsletter 11 | Newsletter 12 |
| | | Whitepaper 1 | | Trade show 1 | Whitepaper 2 | | | Whitepaper 3 | Trade show 2 | | Whitepaper4 | |
| | Emailing | Emailing | Emailing | Emailing | Emailing | Emailing | Emailing | Emailing | Emailing | Emailing | Emailing | Holiday email |
| | New Year's email | | Show release 1 | Show release 2 | | | | Show release 1 | Show release 2 | | | |
| | | | Show email 1 | Show email 2 | Show email 3 | | | Show email 1 | Show email 2 | Show email 3 | | |
| | Article | | | Article | | | Article | | | Article | | |
| | Social media | Social media | Social media | Social media | Social media | Social media | Social media | Social media | Social media | Social media | Social media | Social media |

---

[28] Download the Editorial Calendar template: https://dmcenter.com/track-images-with-inventory-template/editorial-calendar-template

Editorial Calendar – Assignments Tab Headings – 12-month Plan

| Editorial Calendar Template - Content Assignment Calendar | | | | | | | | | | |
|---|---|---|---|---|---|---|---|---|---|---|
| Publication | Publish date | Due date | Author(s) | Topic/Title | Goals/Description | Target | Offer(s) | Keywords | Hashtags | Image |

Your company may commit to the production of white papers and/or articles once a quarter. Articles may involve persuading trade publication editors and getting agreement on issues, particularly during a trade show. White paper production will affect other deadlines for promotional efforts to support those publications.

You can begin to see how scheduling becomes important to nail deadlines for participating authors to meet publication timetables. The same would hold true for videos and other efforts.

Other considerations include seasonal and clearance sales, product updates, industry legislation, personnel changes and partner announcements, holiday messages to thank your customers and partners as well as New Year's resolutions related to the solutions your business offers.

Content planning and creation also takes into consideration advertising materials as well as promotional and sales support materials.

As your team finishes the initial commitments and schedules the materials to be created, develop a spreadsheet, or use project management software, to assign projects and authors by publication with deadlines, description of each item, the goals it must meet, the tone, such as objective vs. subjective, the target group(s), offers and calls-to-action, keywords and hashtags, such as one assigned to a given trade show.

Laying out an entire editorial calendar for all stakeholders lets management and marketing understand assignments in plenty of time to create and deliver great assets. New initiatives will always come up during the year, but activities will be easier to manage and take advantage of new opportunities with a system in place.

**Further reading**
CoSchedule Best 2020 Content Calendar:
https://coschedule.com/blog/annual-content-calendar-template

# Chapter 18

## Types of Content

The good news is that there is a dizzying variety of content to convey messages today. The complexity might seem overwhelming, but project planning and tools help greatly, whether creating pieces that demonstrate thought leadership or urge visitors to buy.

Today's channels reflect the interactive nature of social sharing when companies (Owners) develop content with customers and partners (Shared) or Owners react to User-generated (Audience) comments and reviews, building on the traditional one-sided communications of companies in releases, articles, blog posts and web content.

The purpose of each piece of content drives the appropriate format(s). For instance, educational information from a company can take the form of an ebook, white paper, presentation, article, newsletter

**Examples of Free and Paid Content**

Free
- Blog posts
- Releases
- Articles
- Social media messages

Paid
- Trade magazine ad
- Google Ads
- Social media ads

or webinar to provide substantial value. Those assets then may be promoted by content in other formats: emailings, blog posts, social media, releases or ads.

### Owned (Company-generated content)
### 1. Website
As the cornerstone of a transactional business, your site must provide smooth navigation, immediate comprehension and the fewest clicks to a sales conversion. That's no small order. Another reason for the time commitment to pre-plan every element and sequence of the visitor experience. Copy should be succinct and get to the point expeditiously.

You have only a few seconds to capture attention. Additionally, copy written to the level of an 11-year old garners the highest readability scores, and therefore, the best Google ranking. This environment becomes shared when it allows reviews, comments and testimonials.

## 2. Blog posts

The purpose of a blog post is to communicate one idea in a message between 150 and 1500 words. The idea is to create posts frequently and regularly to earn search engine love. Keywords are a critical part of blog post planning. Select any appropriate hashtags to help draw traffic from promotion elsewhere. Allowing comments on a blog invites interaction with a community.

## 3. Emailings

Emailings are the least expensive form of education and promotion with tremendous potential which also delivers results. Subscribers show interest by signing up, so you must constantly earn their continued loyalty by delivering value. Consider offering previews, coupons and discounts, compelling copy and persuasive calls-to-action. Determine the frequency of delivery carefully; be wary of attrition. Monthly may be just right, weekly perfect for specials and daily only for constantly breaking news.

Email creative should generally be kept to one page. Copy should flow directly to the call-to-action. Don't confuse or distract your audience. Attention-grabbing headlines in the subject fields and instant comprehension are key to successful emailings.

## 4. Newsletters (See Chapter 8)

Newsletters provide in-depth treatment of topics. Often, they include regular columns by author or topic. For instance, a company owner might use a column to discuss current issues affecting customers and the industry. Staff or partners may contribute to featured articles. Most block out a permanent section for product and service promotion, along with links to various parts of the site.

A newsletter template makes these easy to format and email. The initial paragraphs of each article lead to a Read more... with a hyperlink to the full article hosted on the site. Printed newsletters can be shared by sales staff in store locations and at trade shows.

## 5. Articles

Generally 1500 or more words, articles discuss a topic in depth. Consider the audience of the newspaper, site or magazine. Publication should be promoted through the blog, site, emailings, social media and perhaps even press releases. Post summaries with a link to the entire article and edit portions for repurposing, but never repost the identical article.

## 6. White papers

Containing the most academic style of writing, white papers reveal the thought leadership strengths of a company as one of the most valuable assets, while providing strong lead generation stamina. Timing publication prior to events, such as trade shows, is valuable to establish credibility. White papers are promotion-worthy across platforms, can be offered as a download incentive to sign up to newsletters and provided in print form at trade shows and appearances.

Grab the reader's attention: present a problem and an innovative solution quickly. Try to keep the length under 12 pages. Find or create a template to format copy, title page, table of contents, graphics and sources. See Resources at the end of the chapter for free ones.

## 7. Videos

Providing excellent demonstration and testimonial value, video is one of the more dramatic methods to present. YouTube allows you to post videos up to 15 minutes in length. You can then embed them on your site, so visitors can watch without leaving your site. Often, short videos of 1-3 minutes are best. Snippets of videos (30, 60, 90 seconds long) can entice traffic to view the full content as well as standalone in various promotional settings, such as Instagram and emailings.

## Presentations
No longer restricted to slides, visually interesting presentations can educate and motivate an audience to respond. Add narration and music to reuse, or repurpose, as videos.

## 8. Podcasts
Podcasts, like newsletters, require an ongoing commitment to content of substance. Company staff may participate in podcasts hosted by others or choose to record regularly scheduled episodes. Half-hour segments can treat a topic sufficiently and include an interview. Decide whether weekly recording sessions are realistic. Give it a professional look and sound with cover art, an introduction, music and call-to-action.

Make sure you own your own podcast, no matter where you post episodes. Some podcast hosting sites have closed their doors, leaving podcast hosts bereft of their own content. WordPress offers a free PowerPress plugin to fill the bill.

## 9. Collateral
Brochures, sales sheets and other marketing materials related to products and services are not only printed, but also can be available on web pages for download. They should be concise and visually interesting with the appropriate call(s)-to-action.

## 10. Infographics
Powerful graphics illustrating concepts increase the impact of the lesson. Even better, these documents share a great deal of information compactly in one-page units that are easy to share. Find a link to free templates for Infographics in Resources at the end of the chapter.

## 11. Ebooks
Ebooks are a wonderful lead generation offering to urge visitors to sign up for emailings. They can be a mini version of a white paper or any educational topic with a highly perceived value. An ebook is longer than a blog post and shorter than a white paper, depending upon the topic.

The recommended length is 5-20 pages. Consider grouping several related blog posts together.

## 12. Webinars
Webinars provide education as well as thought leadership that increases connections with prospects and customers. These productions offer the opportunity to survey participants, get feedback and end with interactive question and answer periods that benefit both prospect and company. Links to final recorded webinars, posted and emailed, provide continual value. Promoted by email, webinars are a strong lead generation opportunity.

## 13. Press releases
Press releases, while one-sided, often share news with one or more clients, vendors or partners of initiators. The tone of voice must be objective and written in the third person, however, quotes from people involved in the announcements may certainly be subjective. Broadcast to reporters and media in targeted industries and geographies, releases get posted to web sites and shared with customers, prospects and partners.

## 14. Ads
Pay-per-click, such as ads seen on Google, other digital and traditional print, direct mail, radio and TV advertising create remarkable reach across targeted audience segments. Ads obviously come in all sizes and formats. Each requires a compelling call-to-action.

## User-generated content
## 15. Reviews
Web visitors share their opinions about products, services and companies online in reviews. Companies may ask for testimonials and create case studies to use with permission. Activities to encourage positive reviews are important to help improve reputation, search results and meet requirements of pay-per-click platforms. For instance, earning reviews with 3 ½ stars or better is important to be permitted to place ads on Amazon.

### 16. Blog reviews

Many companies work with influencers, who are bloggers with appealing audience profiles, requesting reviews, either paid or free, and with carefully thought-out incentives.

## Shared content (between users and company)
### 17. Comments

On blog posts, Facebook pages, in forums, comments can help or hinder the impressions that the public has regarding a company. Smart businesses monitor and respond to messages, both to thank and apologize with remedies, as needed. Generally, try to delight your audience with messages, perhaps with offers or humor.

### 18. Testimonials and case studies

Companies may ask for testimonials and create case studies to use with permission.

### 19. Polls and surveys

Participants share opinions in public research on sites, social media and webinars which may be published in various venues.

### 20. Social media messages

While company-created messages can be one-sided, the public shares their opinions freely. It's up to companies to manage their reputations with quick response; within an hour is preferred, but certainly within 24 hours. Many companies provide customer service through social media.

Social media messages may be as short as the 280 characters of a tweet; even with this brevity, you can provide links to content of greater value.

## Share content (between media/partners and company)
### 21. Interviews

Company team members may be on panels at trade shows or guests on webinars, interviewed by print and digital publications or podcasters which are terrific opportunities to show thought leadership and wave the company banner. These are shared moments where the company does not have control over what may be asked or stated, so a little coaching goes a long way to represent well.

**Resources**
Always Up-to-Date Guide to Social Media Image Sizes:
https://sproutsocial.com/insights/social-media-image-sizes-guide

Hubspot free templates for white papers and infographics:
https://www.hubspot.com/resources/template

Recommended general digital ad sizes:
https://blog.bannersnack.com/banner-standard-sizes

Readability: https://www.verblio.com/blog/flesch-reading-ease

**Further reading**
The Ultimate White Paper Template [Free Download]:
http://www.curata.com/blog/the-ultimate-white-paper-template-free-download/

How to Write a White Paper Correctly:
https://www.aresearchguide.com/write-a-white-paper.html

Write and publish a free ebook: https://problogger.com/thirteen-steps-to-write-and-publish-a-free-ebook-in-thirteen-hours

How to start a podcast: http://lifehacker.com/how-to-start-your-own-podcast-1709798447

How Long and How Often Should You Podcast:
https://theaudacitytopodcast.com/tap017-how-long-and-how-often-should-you-podcast

4 Steps to Podcasting Success:
https://www.socialmediaexaminer.com/4-steps-to-podcasting-success

# Chapter 19

## Marketing Tools

Choosing the best tools saves small business owners a tremendous amount of precious time while helping to easily increase the numbers of messages, and therefore the increased opportunities for understanding, engagement and action.

Tools come and go frequently and there are tons of them, so a search will find more options as ones mentioned here may not be available in the future. I try to share ones that are likely to be around for a long time to come and/or that I use.

You may well find you have budget and want to purchase the rights to software, images and music. When looking for free stuff, look for trustworthy sources and public domain licenses with the privilege to share, modify and use commercially. Also, beware of suspicious links for free assets that may trigger phishing and damage your computer.

Here are a few of the types of services to make marketing more manageable. Many are free; some offer free trials or a "freemium" model with basic service. Most allow minimal services for free with paid accounts that allow more users and/or more services. I've posted links to the ones that aren't easy to find or obvious; the others are the URL of the name.

**Planning**
**Mindmaps**: Mindmeister
Outline a story or novel, create an organizational chart, diagram parts of a process or business plan with mindmapping software.

**Project management**: Asana, Trello or Wrike
Keeping track of all the moving parts, deadlines and parties is critical to success. Project management software helps you create to do lists,

assign tasks and group teams together in a dashboard format for all users involved.

## Content creation
Free blogging software: WordPress or Blogger
Create a blog or entire site with a free service that provides many additional "plugins" and "widgets" to manage additional helpful tools.

**Free keyword planner:** Google's Keyword Planner vs Ubersuggest[29]
While this is the most obvious choice, Google requires that you set up an Ads account by creating a first ad and entering a credit card number. Assuming you aren't ready, put that first campaign on "pause" to avoid getting charged.

Google's Free Keyword Planner has long been an industry standard, but I find Ubersuggest super easy to use, sharing monthly volume, the SEO difficulty to be found plus the difficulty and cost-per-click for your selected keywords in your paid campaigns.

**Free aggregator:** The Old Reader
Find articles to share with your audience by using an RSS reader to collect and curate content of publications and blogs by industry trade publications and peers.

**Free graphics and creation service:** Canva
Create logos, ads and other images with this free service.

**Free images:** Pixabay
When searching for images for blog posts and your site, always look for appropriate usage rights, such as "free to use, share or modify, even commercially." Choose sources of free images carefully. Bad actors use them for phishing.

**Free music:** SoundCloud, Media College

---

[29] KeywordPlanner: https://adwords.google.com/keywordplanner

Music makes content seem much more professional. Like images, you will want to check the license when you look for free music for YouTube videos, podcasts or presentations. Even royalty-free music will require a one-time payment. Note that YouTube has its own library of free music[30].

**Free fonts:** Google[31]
If you aren't happy with standard fonts and want something special for a logo, scope out these.

**Surveys:** Survey Monkey, Facebook[32], FreeOnlineSurveys.com
Generate credibility with survey results from your customers, team members and partners.

### Promotion & distribution
Free message scheduling service: Buffer[33]
Scheduling messages to various sites from a service, such as Buffer, not only makes posting a month's worth easy, it also tracks multiple users. Platforms also permit direct customer service responses by staff.

### Free URL shortener: Bit.ly
Shortening links is key to messages for Twitter, for instance, since only 280 characters total are allowed. Sometimes a link can be 280 characters, so using a shortener is critical. Hootsuite incorporates one, but I find Bit.ly's is easy to use, especially when creating a lot of links at one time. The shortened length is about 13 characters long. You can customize links for those you use often. Use codes with initials or dates that help you and your audience recognize them quickly.

---

[30] YouTube's music library: https://www.youtube.com/audiolibrary/music
[31] Google fonts: https://fonts.google.com
[32] Facebook Surveys: https://apps.facebook.com/my-surveys
[33] Buffer: find basic free plan at https://buffer.com/pricing/publish

**Email program and marketing automation**: Mail Chimp, Zoho
These two services provide CAN SPAM compliant platforms for free emailing up to 2000 subscribers which top out at 12,000 messages sent per month.

**Free press release software:** PRLog.org, PR.com, PRBuzz.
Distribute your release to search engines, wire services and bloggers with tracking so you can see where releases are posted and pull statistical reports.
Content ideas: Try Social Searcher[34].
Enter a topic to find inspiration or to curate great content.

**Engagement**: LinkedIn Connections in the News
Get email notifications of articles and releases featuring your network of contacts. Imagine the impact when you reach out with a timely reference, perhaps a congratulations or offer.
Go to your profile picture (Me) on LinkedIn, choose Settings & Privacy/Communications/Push/News/Connections mentioned in the news and turn on that function. You will start to get emails when your connections show up in press releases and articles. It will seem instant because they will show up in a day or so of publication.

**Reputation Management:** Google Alerts[35]
Setting up alerts for names of products, companies and individuals or keywords draws emails automatically on chosen topics. Reputation managers search alerts for areas where a quick response can waylay negative comments and get a jump on damage control. In this age of rapid-fire social opinion, it's critical to monitor rumors and negative comments. This activity not only can improve customer service and turnaround poor experiences, but also generate and find positive user-generated content worthy of repurposing.

---

[34] Social Search: https://social-searcher.com
[35] Google Alerts: https://www.google.com/alerts

**Analytics**

**Site statistics**: Google Analytics[36]

Track site traffic and view audience reports for search terms, pages viewed, time spent, audience composition and more. It requires posting a bit of code on your site; find instructions under Help in Analytics or search YouTube for good tutorial.

**Tools**

**Contact management:** Zoho, HubSpot

Sorting lists of prospects, customers, partners and vendors is critical. Lead nurturing works best when prospects are qualified in stages. Contact management software helps to do that and more. Track interactions with prospects and customers by sales and service teams. Create emailings and direct mail campaigns with segmented lists. Both Zoho and Hubspot offer free CRMs, Customer Relationship Management systems. Nonprofits can use Salesforce for free.

**Conference call software:** Zoom, Skype, FreeConferenceCall.com

Perfect for screen-sharing, webinars, recordings or audio calls anywhere.

**Image compression service: Tiny** PNG

To get the best search results, it's important that images load fast on sites. Compression is key. Pick a service that will maintain good resolution.

**Storage:** Google[37], One Drive[38], Dropbox

Photos, videos and web site backups require lots of storage, so know the limits on your account(s). Fifteen gigabytes are often included for free.

---

[36] Google Analytics: https://maketinggplatform/about/analytics
[37] Google drive: https://drive.google.com
[38] One Drive: https://onedrive.live.com

**Monetization**
Search ads: Google AdSense[39], YouTube
Select the format and size ads. Choose pages to accept ads and implement code. Check results and modify to improve results.

**Affiliate programs:** CJ Affiliate[40], ShareASale, Pepperjam, LinkShare
Sign up, choose ads, get links and post. Each affiliate network offers 24/7 reporting and monthly automatic payment.

**Further reading**
Compilation of free software for small business:
http://fitsmallbusiness.com/free-small-business-software/

Curata's Content Marketing Tools Ultimate List:
http://www.contentcurationmarketing.com/ultimate-list-of-curation-tools

The 7 Best Free Social Media Management Tools:
https://www.wordstream.com/blog/ws/2018/01/17/best-free-social-media-management-tools

Google analytics tutorial [Video]:
https://www.youtube.com/watch?v=mm78xlsADgc

Google Analytics: First Steps:
https://www.youtube.com/watch?v=mm78xlsADgc

Navigate Google analytics [Video]
https://www.youtube.com/watch?v=I7YA1oZhevo

Compression tools: https://www.3ptechies.com/reduce-image-size-online-quickly-7-best-free-tools-for-optimal-image-compression.html

---

[39] Google Adsense: https://www.google.com/adsense/start
[40] CJ Affiliate, now part of Publicis Groupe: https://cj.com

Eight Free Online Image Compression Services Tested:
https://www.motocms.com/blog/en/free-online-image-compression-services

20+ free press release services: http://mashable.com/2007/10/19/press-releases/#1GVi69aCrGq3

# Phase III

## Go! Promotion —Free and Paid

Step through various methods of promotion from free marketing services to paid, moving gradually into the next more expensive channel, all while making sure each new channel is micro-managed profitably.

The first pages (Go: Free) deal with promotion you can do for free. All companies, big and small, should take maximum advantage of social media. I've had several companies tell me they never need to advertise again because they get plenty of leads from social media and organic (free) search results leading to their sites.

The following section (Go: Paid) starts with the least expensive channels, showing how each is used by performance-based marketers successfully.

**Key takeaway**
Have the patience to give each channel a fair test before adding the next. Tweak creative, monitor, analyze performance and retest until you get the desired results.

# Chapter 20

## Engagement

Today's marketer not only supervises creation of company-owned messaging, but also user-generated content (UGC).

The responsibility to monitor UGC isn't taken lightly. Proactively jumping on comments to diffuse a PR situation reduces the clean-up effort. On the other hand, taking advantage of the opportunity to collect and repurpose rave reviews expeditiously hits a home run.

### What it takes to convert

Success depends upon your ability to shepherd attention to purpose, choice of target audience, call-to-action, tone of voice, scheduling, distribution, reputation and budget management.

### Purpose

The intent of your message and placement will drive other decisions. For instance, educational materials must be more objective than self-promotional pieces. Readers presume collateral materials will boast about company strengths, but when it comes to white papers, they expect serious, objective presentations.

### Target audience

A review of your market and reader profile for each specific placement will guide your target audience(s) which, in turn, will induce the voice for each message. Consider all your different prospective audiences: a decision-maker may not be the end user, for example. A white paper might be targeted at CXO level executives rather than support staff, so the writing would be tailored to be receptive to that audience.

### Call-to-action

Decide what action(s) you want your audience to take with each marketing piece. Whatever the transaction, registration or download, you'll make the best use of your efforts and achieve the best ROI to craft the shortest, smoothest transition to your desired result.

## Tone of voice

Each channel's profile, coupled with your corporate approach, e.g. professional and authoritative vs. quirky and fun, will dictate writing style. A press release, for instance, must be objective and third party, while a blog post is typically less formal, subjective and may tell a story.

## Scheduling, frequency and distribution

Most messages can be scheduled to be posted ahead of time, easing time management. Don't annoy your prospects by hounding them repeatedly with the same, self-promotional or boring messages. The rule of thumb in social media is to promote yourself only once for every ten messages. Additionally, be careful with distribution so you reach your intended audience. For example, when posting on Facebook or LinkedIn you may choose select groups or public distribution of your message. Press releases are another opportunity to choose geographical, trade industry and other circulation.

## Sharing

Encourage followers to share content—both theirs and yours. Get permission and share their user-generated content.

## Monitoring

Social media presents new opportunities for advertisers to enjoy the praises of customers and reviewers because of the viral nature of sharing with their followers. Everything from liking a page or a message, rave review or comment all accumulate impressions that linger a long time. This crowd credibility goes the distance to persuade their friends to follow, engage and buy.

## Reputation

While you no longer have complete control over messages about your firm, you can create procedures to help avoid PR nightmares. Website visitors can make or break a company's reputation. That's why monitoring and timely response is so critical. Your site, blog and social media that allow comments must be assigned to staff for constant review of every mention and speedy, accurate, satisfying answers. These answers have the potential to turn unhappy customers into advocates and defuse potentially viral complaints.

## Budget
Much of the content that is produced can be done with a little time. Many services to post and schedule are free. Costs can be minor, such as a few hundred dollars to use one of the better press release services. Monitoring and creative services require estimates. Paid advertising and sponsored content certainly take analysis for potential audience size and ROI to make good choices and close approximations for testing and rollout.

The Conversation Prism table[41] details different types of content and considerations for purpose, tone of voice, authorship, credibility, paid vs. free content, whether the content is aimed at retailers and scheduling capabilities.

## Further reading
Yelp vs. Google vs. Facebook Review: which should you focus on and why? https://searchenginewatch.com/2016/09/19/yelp-vs-google-vs-facebook-reviews-which-should-you-focus-on-and-why

38 mind blowing stats about user-generated content: https://www.tintup.com/blog/38-mind-blowing-stats-effectiveness-user-generated-content

---

[41] ConversationPrism.com

# Chapter 21

## Acquisition and retention

Marketers spend a lot of time planning steps and methods to acquire and retain customers. Acquisition, the art and science to capture a lead and eventually a sale, and retention, the series of activities involved in keeping each hard-won customer, are critical to maximize revenues over the consumer life cycle.

Business-to-business (B2B) as well as business-to-consumer (B2C) campaigns both benefit from lead nurturing, not only before the initial sale, but also ongoing through future sales. Most departments get involved in the variety of touches. Beyond just sales and marketing, product development and customer service also own a stake in these relationships. Product development, for instance, may offer surveys or new product testing. Customer service works hard to help solve issues of product, shipping and billing satisfaction; even offering further discounts, products and services.

### Acquisition

It often takes 7-14 touches to solicit web visitor actions, whether a sale, donation or registration. That's why patience and planning pay off.

Acquiring a first connection may occur through word-of-mouth, social referrals, reviews, releases, digital or print articles at no cost. However, it's extremely difficult to build significant sales without advertising, such as paid traditional marketing through TV, print, radio or direct mail advertising. Eventually, companies generating good content and interactions may reduce their dependence on advertising.

A completed sale often requires multiple messages. The more expensive and complicated the product/service, the longer acquisition takes. That's why capturing initial contact information is so crucial. Emailings and customer service through live chat are examples of methods used to secure purchases and other actions.

Acquisition through advertising is the most expensive way drive sales. That's why retention, the development of further sales from customers, is so important to profitability.

**Retention**
Acquiring customers is 5-25x more expensive than the cost to retain one. Every customer retained is worth 9 new ones. Consider that the average loss of customers, or churn rate, is 10-25%. Imagine losing every customer in just four years! What's more, the retention of 5% of customers generates 95-125% more profit.

Why is that?
1. Repeat customers spend 33% more on subsequent purchases
2. Previous customers have confidence
3. Previous customers are less sensitive to prices

Moreover, retaining 10% more customers can increase company value by 30%. Loyal customers tell friends about good experiences.

Retention activities help companies learn more about what customers like and don't like. Unhappy customers will tell 17 friends; social media spreads their discontent further. Surveys, monitoring and interactions of social media messages and community forums by customer service staff contribute to data analysis.

Prepare strategies to resolve issues expeditiously. Establish procedures to rescue sales from shopping cart abandonment. Then, empower and train call center staff. Use CRM and marketing automation tools. Enable live chat services to handle queries quickly. Create and update a thorough set of FAQs regularly.

Check in regularly with customers to provide education, discounts, coupons, events, free trials, reports and special previews to reward and deepen loyalty. Ask for referrals; word-of-mouth recommendations, such as reviews, carry tremendous authority and credibility.

In this example of 16 possible touches during the life cycle of a customer, you can see how various content is scheduled across media to create a steady flow that encourages action and interaction. Actions 1,2,7, and 16 are acquisitions and the rest are retention activities.

1. A prospect sees a TV commercial and goes to a web site
2. Prospect clicks on a link to collect a promised ebook
3. The thank-you landing page for downloading the ebook offers a 10% discount off a first purchase for signing up to receive emails
4. A thank-you email for signing up for the newsletter offers more free downloads
5. The customer selects a free mini course with 5 daily emails
6. Email follow-up reminds customer of shopping cart abandonment
7. A retargeted ad captures new purchase
8. At the site, the customer is encouraged to use live chat
9. A post-purchase thank-you email presents a membership incentive w/ special promo code
10. A follow-up email confirms shipment, arrival date and tracking link
11. The next email asks about satisfaction, requests a review and provides a link
12. An unopened email is followed up by an automatic resend with a new subject line
13. A personalized direct mail piece after 3 months of inactivity provides a new uniquely priced offer
14. A customer service call is placed re: satisfaction with autoship discount offer for item previously bought
15. A follow-up survey offers an incentive to get special previews on Facebook
16. A Facebook ad generates a new purchase

As businesses add further channels of promotion and advertising, the possibilities increase for further sales and a higher average order value.

**Further reading**

What is Retention Marketing and Why You Need to Start Today: https://blog.hubspot.com/marketing/what-is-retention-marketing-why-you-need-to-start

Six Retention Marketing Strategies: https://neverbounce.com/blog/6-relationship-marketing-strategies-for-higher-customer-retention

# Chapter 22

## Campaign management

Continual improvement of marketing campaigns and sales tactics based on data analysis helps companies today respond more quickly to customer needs and makes the most of their time and budget. Companies achieve the requisite competitive edge by analyzing audience and actions with 24/7 accuracy, assessing engagement and influence with data visualization tools.

Statistics from your website and social media pages include audience demographics, interests, where web visitors come from and where they go next. Measurements track actions; leads, sales, donations, subscribers, downloads and more.

Ecommerce and customer relationship management (CRM) platforms, email marketing automation, Google Analytics, email, blogs, PR, social media and proprietary reporting tools all aid in pulling together results. Set up report formats and review statistics regularly to take advantage of opportunities that maximize ROI. Many services are free or include a free basic level. They'll also integrate with other software easily and are excellent choices for small business.

Google Analytics reports site traffic and insights into web visitors. Format data from Google Ads, DoubleClick, YouTube and other social media. See Further Reading at end of chapter to get instructions to set up Google Analytics.

Expect an ecommerce platform to offer reports across sales, inventory, shipping, returns, finances, taxes, visitor behavior and conversion performance. Shopify[42], for instance, has a neat dashboard overview.

---

[42] Shopify: https://help.shopify.com/manual/reports-and-analytics/shopify-reports/store-dashboard

CRM services, such as Zoho[43], allow companies to track interactions with customers. Sales teams document progress from lead to sale; agents report customer calls, responses and follow-up actions; marketing staff create email campaigns synced with email delivery programs.

MailChimp[44] offers a CAN SPAM compliant emailing service to automate promotional, cart abandonment and other messages as well as a free version. Pull performance statistics to review delivery, open and click-through rates.

Additionally, other software, such as enterprise resource planning (ERP) which helps manage back-office functions as well as content, affiliate program, project management software and social media management might also facilitate results reporting and analysis. All-in-one business dashboards, such as Cyfe[45], integrate statistics from many different platforms.

As new situations arise, add fields to track and aggregate statistics together. Weekly reports are important, but you may review digital stats on demand to see how new campaigns trend. Monthly, quarterly and annual summaries give perspective for projections.

Start by setting up a report of benchmarks[46] for the metrics to be tracked: site, blog, emailings, sales conversions, numbers of leads, sales, donations, subscribers, downloads, engagement and influence. Test new products, prices or formats, get answers to improve results, revise and rollout.

---

[43] Zoho: https://www.zoho.com
[44] MailChiimp: https://mailchimp.com/
[45] Cyfe: https://www.cyfe.com/
[46] Benchmark templates: dmcenter.com/marketing-success-track-trends-analytics/benchmarks-2

**Further reading**
Google Analytics Academy: Free courses:
https://analytics.google.com/analytics/academy
Analytics sign up:
https://analytics.google.com/analytics/web/?authuser=0#provision/SignUp

# Chapter 23

## Go! Promotion: Paid

Advertising can be added to the mix once every free promotional avenue, such as social media, press releases and articles, is mastered. Choose paid methods wisely: 1) to get the biggest bang for the budget and 2) to select media that best deliver the message and target group. Next, do an effective job with each before adding the next. That means generally starting with least expensive media before gradually testing the more expensive ones, which is why I've laid these out in order.

### Media budgeting and planning

No matter how much money a company has budgeted, it behooves each to create and follow both a marketing plan (what efforts do we want to address this year?) and a media plan (specifically which media will we schedule to attract what audience and/or meet what sales goals?). Planning should coordinate both free promotion and paid advertising activities.

Consider duration of promotions, seasonality, demographics, psychographics and geography of your target audience. Set goals to meet or exceed minimum goals to reach targets with some frequency.

### Reach and frequency

It's important to do a sufficient job of reaching enough of a target audience to decide whether a schedule of media is successful or not. Generally, the concept of reaching over half a target audience in a specific geographic area and often enough to make an impact might mean a goal of 60% reach with a minimum 3x frequency. Multiply the reach times the message frequency (60x3) to get the number of rating points, (one rating point is 1% of the audience), which yields 180 points. In a radio buy, these 180 points may air across 3 different stations. An entire mixed media campaign may be given a reach and frequency goal over a given geography, say a two-county area or one of Nielsen's

Designated Market Areas (DMAs), a method of assigning every U.S. county to one of 210 marketing geographies.

## Choosing media

Features and benefits as well as cost should be considered when selecting a medium. For instance, products that require demonstration would use visual media, such as television and print. Marketers choose radio to tell a story. Each has its drawbacks: formats may be very short in length or challenging to generate and measure responses.

## Measurement: negotiation and analysis

Speaking of measurement, numbers are used to evaluate and negotiate media as well as to track leads and sales results. Buyers initially select media by comparing audience statistics across similar units. Once media airs, advertisers divide the total media cost by the number of leads or orders received for a given set of dates, known as a flight.

## Media purchasing and negotiation

Units such as cost-per-thousand (CPM) and cost-per-point (CPP) help media buyers choose most media. CPM is the cost to reach 1,000 audience members; CPP is the cost to reach 1% of a target group. Search marketing uses cost-per-click (CPC) comparisons, reviewing the cost for one visitor to click a web link. Buyers review media vehicles and time slots, such as examining morning drive time CPMs or CPPs for the same target in the same market and geography. Then they negotiate based on the lowest metric, CPP or other, to meet or beat budget goals.

Media sales representatives have internal goals to receive the greater portion of ad dollars for each campaign. In broadcast sales, for instance, buyers can leverage giving a larger share to a station in order to receive lower rates.

In general, offering more budget helps to drive down unit prices; accepting a longer-term contract for advertising earns lower rates, for instance.

Some media buyers may contract for a full year's worth of ads at one time, knowing they can make changes and cancel as agreed upon. A cancellation clause might stipulate a two-week notice. Changes might include revising scheduled publication or air dates, positioning or time slots, ad sizes or lengths.

## Discounts
In addition to volume discounts, agencies, including in-house agencies, earn as much as 15% commission. Some media allow a 2% cash discount for payment by a certain date, such as on the 15th day of the following month. Advertisers without a credit history or buying infomercial time must pay in advance; those earning credit get 30-day terms. While agencies typically make 15%, those rates may be negotiated with clients.

## Media results analysis
Marketers analyze results by comparing the cost to receive an order (CPO) or lead (CPL) over any single medium and any campaign time frame (daily, weekly, etc.). Regular review leads to campaign revisions to constantly improve results.

## Making advertising accountable
Direct marketing, also called direct response, tracks clicks, leads and/or sales, using unique devices, such as links, coupon or promo codes and/or toll-free numbers to measure success. Success dictates which elements are bought again.

Some built-in measurement captures an email address or a completed form by webinar or trade show attendees in direct response. Use promo codes or easy-to-remember unique URL or 800 numbers to help track results.

## Direct response strategy: test/tweak/rollout
Direct response by design makes the most of every dollar spent. The process minimizes risk by testing creatives with budgets just large enough to get reliable results. Analysis of results drives the next

purchase which may be another test, for instance, in the case where price point or creative are changed. Once tweaks generate a good return, then rollout begins. Rollouts are done cautiously, retaining the strategy to continue to test new elements gradually. When results drop, media slots are put on hiatus and retested later.

Products that are impulse items generate the greatest response, while items offering prevention or security are more of a creative challenge. Items with a low price point where the benefits are simple to explain do well. More expensive products and services or ones where the benefits are more difficult to explain require a two-step method where leads are gathered to nurture and close.

## $ (Least Expensive Paid Advertising)
## Digital advertising

### $ Affiliate marketing
I prefer performance-based advertising because I'm interested in the return on investment. Marketers give a fixed cost-per-sale to affiliated sites that run ads on web pages, in newsletters, with search marketing or even by a pay-per-call method.
Creative formats may include digital display, datafeeds, emailings, text links and more. Digital ads scheduled to retarget visitors appear on other sites; some run in social media.

### $ Search marketing
Pay-per-click is potentially the next most efficient advertising method, by persuading web visitors to click on links from keyword search results. Google's Ads (formerly Google AdWords) and YouTube both offer powerful platforms. For products, Amazon's impact is growing quickly.

### $ Social media advertising
Just $50/day can yield results in a few days to determine whether continuing would be worthwhile. Campaigns can be turned on or off instantly with 24/7 reporting.

Facebook, Instagram, Pinterest and Twitter all accept ads in different formats. A little digging turns up guidance to target geographically and by demographics to get the best results.

## $$ (More expensive)

### $$ Direct mail

Consumers receive a lot fewer pieces of direct mail today which averages a 5% response rate, the highest ever recorded, which opens an opportunity for businesses to make an impact. Certainly, a powerful CTA and compelling creative play critical parts in getting a profitable response.

### $$ Print

Advertising in newspapers continues to be effective, especially for elderly target groups. Both magazines and newspapers offer digital components which may be bought together or separately.

### $$ Radio

Local market radio delivers geographic targeting efficiently, generally in metropolitan areas. Radio stations can provide a visual component to content with their websites. Advertisers rely on a message length generally twice as long as the average TV spot.

## $$$ (Even more expensive)

### $$$ Television

Local market television also delivers audiences beyond radio with a visual as well as audio platform for messages. Additionally, TV stations devote digital content to sites that may be bought in combination or separately.

**$$$$ (Most expensive)**

**$$$$ Network TV and radio**
While network and syndicated television and radio advertising cost the most, they also have the greatest coverage per unit. These also offer advertising opportunities on their digital platforms.

**$$-$$$$**

**Sponsorships and trade shows**
Historically, companies advertised to build their brand recognition with direct mail, print, radio or TV. Many use sponsorships and trade shows to demonstrate commitment to an industry, program or a charity, which can be large expenditures with results that aren't as easy to measure as other methods.

**Further reading**
Direct      mail      response      rates:      https://compu-mail.com/blog/2017/07/14/30-direct-mail-statistics-for-2017

# Chapter 24

## Affiliate Marketing

### Affiliate marketing guarantees ROI

Performance-based affiliate marketing lets online advertisers gain sales and leads at the fixed cost per sale or lead of their choice. It's no wonder, then, that approximately 80% of advertisers in a Forrester study allot 10% of their marketing budget to their affiliate programs. Moreover, half of them generate 20% of their revenues with this method. Forrester estimates an average 10% increase per year to $6.8 billion[47] in affiliate program spending by 2020. Forrester advertiser quote source in footnote.[48]

> "We've seen that affiliate is one of our best ROI channels. It yields more revenue for our .com property than SEM, display or social. We always invest in the most efficient channel first."
> -Advertiser in Forrester survey[48]

Affiliate programs aggregate thousands of websites to sell products and services for merchants, accounting for 16% of online revenue[49]. Like search marketing, affiliate programs work best when supporting offline advertising efforts and brand name products.

Advertisers post a description, its payout and marketing assets in a software program that generates trackable links to give each website proper credit as well as payments. These systems provide both advertisers, known as merchants, and websites, known as publishers, 24/7 access to all statistics.

---

[47] Forrester: http://www.marketingdive.com/news/why-affiliate-marketing-is-a-growing-opportunity-for-advertisers/415078/

[48] Forrester advertiser in survey:
http://blog.marketing.rakuten.com/hubfs/Networks_Help_Drive_Affiliate_Marketing_Into_The_Mainstream.pdf

[49] Internet Retailer: https://www.internetretailer.com/commentary/2016/03/20/3-myths-about-affiliate-marketing

Advertisers may choose software to run the program internally and/or choose one or more affiliate networks to do so. In-house software manages proprietary company affiliate relationships. Affiliate networks offer access to tens of thousands of site publishers.

Networks charge 2-3% of the sale on top of the revenues the affiliates earn, not only providing the platform, but actively recruiting and promoting programs as well as monitoring affiliates for fraudulent activity.

Conversant (formerly Commission Junction or CJ), the largest of these with 75,000 publishers and 3,000 merchants, costs the most in set-up and may have requirements, such as $1 million in online sales. You'll have to complete the application process to get the answer for your situation.

Others to consider include Pepperjam, LinkShare and the smallest, ShareASale (14,000 publishers), where set-up costs are lower. Publisher duplication across these networks ranges between 80-98%. There are a few dozen other networks, but these are the main ones to discuss at the outset. ShareASale, as the least expensive platform, is best for beginners.

Advertisers can provide a variety of assets for websites to choose from: textlinks, banner ads, datafeeds, search marketing and email creatives.

As a rule, 20% of affiliates generate 80% of revenues, so it's important to develop relationships to get additional and more prominent exposure. Advertisers create custom creatives, promotions and offer higher payouts for top performers.

**Outsourced affiliate program management (OPMs)**
Hiring a manager makes sense to realize a program's true potential. It takes several months and effort to nurture recruits to post assets. They are responsible to monitor activities daily to react quickly to results, fraud and spam while generating status reports regularly. OPM services

start at about $1500/month and may also take a performance fee of approximately 3%.

## Affiliate marketing creative options
To appeal to the greatest number of websites, create a wide variety of ad versions, such as:
1. Textlinks: Text copy up to 150 characters in length with a hyperlink to a landing page
2. Banner ads: These are generally accepted formats: 728x90, 300x250, 160x600, 120x600, 468x60, 234x60, 120x120, 120x90, 120x60, 125x125, 100x100 and 88x31. Banners should be no more than 60K in size and be done in .GIF or .JPG formats only. Banners, where space is available, should always have a call to action- even a simple "click here" works. In addition, some movement/animation is preferred in the banners as long as the file size is not exceeded. A simple flashing "click here" is sufficient.
3. Datafeed: The fields in a datafeed spreadsheet populate product details to websites, including image URLs, price, features, SKU and more.
4. Email marketing
5. Coupons
6. Loyalty/rewards
7. Search marketing
8. Reviews
9. Pay per call (lead generation) by IVR technology or live operators

## Resources
WordPress Affiliate Platform Plugin: https://www.tipsandtricks-hq.com/wordpress-affiliate-platform-plugin-simple-affiliate-program-for-wordpress-blogsite-1474

The Essential Affiliate Marketing Glossary of Terms: https://www.mobidea.com/academy/affiliate-marketing-glossary

# Chapter 25

## Digital media placement

The formats for ads and digital media images have exploded in recent years, offering lots of new opportunities for testing.

### Affiliate marketing (Chapter 24)

The most profitable form of digital media advertising is affiliate marketing, a form of performance marketing, where companies set the price that they are willing to pay for a sale or a lead. Upload a wide variety of ads of different sizes to appeal to the greatest number of publishers and for multiple placements on any one site.

### Search marketing

While Google's Ads (formerly AdWords) program and Facebook are the big gorillas in pay-per-click advertising, Bing, Yahoo, Amazon, Snapchat and Twitter should not be overlooked. Google includes YouTube and the Doubleclick display ad network while Facebook includes Instagram.

Keywords are the foundations for all things search: both optimization and pay-per-click. Optimization is the process to attract web visitors by using keywords in copy and links both onsite and off while keeping tight reins on technical site issues, developing fresh content and nurturing links from relevant domains. The cost for optimization is generally just the time of internal staff. Pay-per-click marketing, either text or display, draws targeted web traffic to site landing pages through intricate online campaigns of keywords, phrases and groups of word strings. Advertisers generally pay a bid price for each click a visitor makes.

Create a campaign in the platform(s) of choice. Determine the maximum daily expenditure for a test. Since pay-per-click campaigns offer 24/7 results reporting, it's possible to turn campaigns on and off instantly. A test of a few days or one week can demonstrate whether an offer has legs. It takes very little money too: just $50/day in a local market on Facebook generates enough activity to determine success. If successful, expand the campaign; if not, regroup, rewrite, resubmit and retest.

Amazon Advertising is the pay-per-click service for your offerings on Amazon. While the overall concept is like Google Ads, Amazon does not do groups of keywords when running a campaign. There are many other differences related to selling on Amazon. But, word to the wise regarding both Google and Amazon, don't break their rules or you'll be sorry. Neither is easy to work with and with enough budget, it's best to hire a pro.

### Retargeting and remarketing
Oftentimes these words are used interchangeably to refer to a pixel-based method that triggers ads to web visitors once they have left a site. Many use the word remarketing to discuss list-based efforts, generally through email marketing, to continue to send messages to visitors. Google, however, uses the term remarketing for its ad serving services post-web visits and charge a per-click price.

The term remarketing is also used to describe email nurturing of prospects and past purchasers.

### Digital assets
Here are several popular digital ad sizes to prepare:
- Leaderboard ads, which usually appear on the top of a site, perhaps at middle or bottom, measuring 728x90 pixels
- A medium rectangle, measuring 300x250 pixels, a popular size
- Skyscrapers:
  160x600, a wide skyscraper seen at the side of a webpage
  120x600, skyscraper
- Banners:
  468x60, a basic horizontal banner size
  234x60, also known as a half banner
- Buttons: 120x90, 120x60, 125x125, 120x120 100x100, known as square buttons and 88x31, known as a micro bar

**Video**
30 or 60 seconds long for most purposes

**Digital ad sizes**
Textlinks, videos and datafeeds are two other types of materials that advertisers should prepare. Textlinks are short phrases that use hyperlinked text to send visitors to landing pages while datafeeds include information about products ranging from descriptions, images, prices and landing page links to populate an affiliate's web page.

View pictures of 3 basic sizes at
http://www.knowonlineadvertising.com/facts-about-online-advertising/common-sizes-of-ads.

**Mobile ad sizes:**
320X480
300X400
300X250

320X480 is the most popular size and allows for more context, clearer call to action and more creative content like videos, store locator etc.

**Native ads**, placed within other written material resemble the publication's content, come in various forms and sizes. Native ads are viewed 53% more often than banners. They are less intrusive than banners for mobile advertising, have a higher click thru rate, better ad engagement and an improved user experience. LinkedIn is one venue that offers Native ads.

**Google ads**
Find specs and file types for various Google display ads at https://support.google.com/google-ads/answer/1722096?hl=en: Social Media Ads

## Facebook

Facebook's low cost to test makes it an attractive choice. Find ad specs for feed, carousel, right-column, in-stream, sponsored and more at https://sproutsocial.com/insights/facebook-ad-sizes.

## LinkedIn

LinkedIn's professional audience may cost more, but also is more targeted for B2B advertisers. Ad specs for sponsored, carousel, display and more are found at https://www.linkedin.com/help/lms/topics/8340/8341.

## Twitter

Here's a set of specifications for Twitter ads at https://business.twitter.com/en/help/campaign-setup/advertiser-card-specifications.html.

## YouTube

Get YouTube ad specs at https://www.cpcstrategy.com/blog/2019/02/youtube-ad-specs.

## Instagram

Find specs for image, video, Stories and carousel ad sizes at https://sproutsocial.com/insights/instagram-ad-sizes.

## Size matters

The file size for banners should be no more than 60K in size and be done in .GIF or .JPG formats only. Note the file size for the 200x200 pixel ad is only 12kb as a .jpg.

| Name | Size | Type | File Size |
|------|------|------|-----------|
| Generic ad | 200x200 | JPG | 12 KB |
| Generic ad2 | 200x200 | PNG | 24 KB |

As always, include a call to action. Use animation, but mind file size limits.

**Further reading**

Get Pinterest and Snapchat specs too. Raka promises an always up-to-date guide of ad specs: https://www.rakacreative.com/blog/digital-advertising/display-ad-sizes-an-always-up-to-date-guide

What Video Ad Length is Best on Facebook: https://www.emarketer.com/Article/What-Video-Ad-Length-Best-on-Facebook/1014438

# Chapter 26

## Direct mail

Personalizing a letter or selecting an oversized postcard can make a memorable, compelling impact in an age when consumers receive less snail mail. The increased response rate of direct mail to 5%, the highest since reporting started in 2003, according to a 2017 report by the Direct Marketing Association (DMA), makes this channel more appealing. One of the reasons for the uptick might be a decline in overall mailbox clutter, due to the prevalence of email.

Small businesses use special offers and simple eye-popping graphics to develop new customer interest while regaining top-of-mind awareness with past store and web visitors. Oversized cards (8.52"x 4.57") stand out from normal business mail consumers receive, offering a wonderful opportunity to make a significant graphic statement.

Estimate costs for creative, printing, postage and any list rentals. Keep the message simple with a clear call-to-action. A direct agency firm can lay out options for attention-getting creative with paper stock choices to earn the most efficient postage cost. A qualified list mailing house will rent lists scrubbed to remove names from The Association of National Advertiser's (ANA) national opt-out Mail Preference Service (MPS). Mail houses and other vendors handle returns and update lists unless you want to keep those activities in-house. Members of the ANA agree to remove names that are on the MPS list when mailing to honor consumer wishes, setting the good practices standard for the advertising industry.

Three-dimensional pieces, ones arriving in boxes, tubes or padded envelopes have a higher response rate than flat pieces and are often worth the greater cost, especially for products and services with a longer sales cycle requiring a significant customer investment.

**Further reading**
Direct mail response rate: https://compu-mail.com/blog/2017/07/14/30-direct-mail-statistics-for-2017

How to Choose the Best B2B List [white paper] from Beasley Direct: https://beasleydirect.com/white_papers/how-to-select-an-accurate-b2b-list

# Chapter 27

## Print advertising

Print advertising is often negotiable, generally illustrating sliding scales on published rate cards for purchases made in volume and frequency. Many newspapers and magazines won't negotiate, but the effort is always worth a try.

### Print overview

To evaluate print choices, buyers use circulation information to see how a publication's audience is distributed through counties or metropolitan areas. This coverage, audited independently, can be compared across publications and then against media costs for ads of equal size. Publications often provide demographic, occupation, income and behavioral statistics.

Newspapers and magazines generally prepare annual editorial calendars to announce topics for stories in upcoming months that buyers use to choose appropriate issues. Special sections provide opportunities of interest. For instance, newspapers have a Best Food Day and Sunday supplements in addition to ongoing sections for news, sports and lifestyle content as well as classifieds.

Typically, buyers negotiate by comparing the cost to reach 1,000 of their audience, such as households. Agencies and media sales representatives have access to software to pull audience reports for reach and frequency of demographics and psychographics. SRDS (Standard Rate and Data Service) publishes information about newspapers, business and consumer magazines (as well as other media). Publishers and agencies purchase the online SRDS service, but the books are found in the library reference section.

Ad agencies are allowed a 15% discount and some media vehicles allow a 2% cash discount for speedy payment. Advertisers submit credit applications for approval to secure terms.

Both newspapers and magazines go beyond print to offer digital and often email newsletters.

### Creative assets
Display rate cards (as opposed to classified rates) will specify types of ad sizes, such as full page, ½ page, ¼ page and the like for the main sections of publications. Ads are measured in columns across and vertical inches. Buyers choose black and white (B&W) or four-color (4C, sometimes referred to as full color) and provide what is called camera-ready art. Most publications request media be uploaded to a site used by their layout department.

### Digital assets
As an example, USA Today's rate card[50] spells out details for digital specifications for formats in audio, video, logos for desktop to mobile.

### Positioning
Buyers request positions and pay to fix certain positions for their ads. Upper right-hand page positions in a certain section (such as news, sports or leisure), for instance, might be important. Rate cards offer pricing for the most prized placements, such as inside front right-hand page or back outside page.

### Insertion orders
Known as insertion order, contracts provide the publication dates, requested or paid positions, cost based on a sliding scale with volume (number of ads), agency and/or cash discount rates, advertiser media buyer, billing and tear sheet contact information at the client, reference number and any other instructions. Make sure to check any vendor contracts immediately upon receipt for correctness to avoid disputes.

---

[50] USA Today rate card: http://marketing.usatoday.com/wp-content/uploads/2015/07/2017-Rate-Card-Final-01-18-v3.pdf

## Cancellation clause

Make note of cancellation clauses. Don't expect publications to waive these rules.

## Deadline

When reviewing the rate card, be sure to note the deadlines both for the insertion order and for copy and stick to them. Don't count on the kindness of an extension.

## Proof

When magazines and newspapers provide proofs of creative to be approved, make sure to give a timely response.

## Tear sheets

Check and measure every tear sheet, or proof of ad publication, carefully. These may not necessarily arrive with the invoice. Coordinate with internal billing department to approve all tear sheets and invoices prior to payment.

## Makegoods

If an ad's publication doesn't run or meet the insertion order requirements, a buyer may negotiate a discount or "makegood," a new publication date and prepare a revised insertion order with a new date.

## Remnant or direct response print

Remnant print advertising is often substantially lower in cost, often 50% or even 70% less, based on the advertiser's willingness to have their ad dropped in only at the last minute. There is always the possibility that the ad won't be published. Marketers provide their creative for approval in the event a spot becomes available and they don't get much notice.

Advertisers who use remnant print often estimate and plan that 20-50% of their ads may not run and may overbook based on print vehicles' history of preemption, likely to be higher in fourth quarter for the Christmas season, for instance. Should all ads run, marketers must have budget ready for all additional expenditures.

**Results tracking**

As always, use specific calls-to-action, directing readers to a link and/or phone number with a trackable functionality, such as a promo code.

**Further reading**

Understanding newspaper rate cards:
https://www.thebalance.com/understanding-advertising-rate-cards-2890304

Example of magazine rate card: http://marketing.usatoday.com/wp-content/uploads/2016/05/Materials-Info-Guide-05-09-16.pdf

Example of newspaper rate cards
The Daily Courier:
http://www.thedailycourier.com/pdfs/dispratecard.pdf
Washington Journey:
http://www.aaawashingtonjourney.com/pdf/MediaKit/MediaKit2017-Print.pdf

Example of materials specifications in rate card:
http://marketing.usatoday.com/wp-content/uploads/2016/05/Materials-Info-Guide-05-09-16.pdf

# Chapter 28

## Radio

Sales from radio advertising yields $6 for every $1 in advertising expenditures, making it perhaps the most successful ROI of any medium.

Radio time is available not only on traditional network and local AM and FM terrestrial stations, but also through satellite, such as Sirius XM, as well as streamed through podcasting and music platforms. Broadcast radio networks, such as NBC News Radio and CBS Sports Radio, produce their own programming. "On Air with Ryan Seacrest" is an example of a syndicated radio show (not made specifically for a network).

Since radio doesn't have the visual opportunity of television, commercials are typically 60 seconds long, as opposed to the normal 30-second TV spot, in order to allow messages to sink in. AM radio station signals mostly cover metro areas, but there are a few 50,000-watt stations whose signals broadcast to large regions of the U.S. FM stations may sell commercial time slots in combination with AM time from the same ownership. Sirius provides a platform for national exposure, often chosen for a specific personality's show or specialized content.

Radio commercials, also known as spots, are sold in dayparts, such as morning and afternoon drive time. The narrower the time segment, the higher the price; therefore, allowing commercials to run within a broad time period rotation, even Run of Station (ROS), where spots may air between Monday and Sunday and between 6AM to midnight, costs far less.

Buyers also review time slots aired to ensure an even distribution through a time period, also called a fair rotation. A buyer who purchases four spots between 6AM and 10AM expects that one will run in each hour. If they all run in the hour with the smallest audience of the rotation, the buyer should use that result in a negotiation for a makegood or future buy. Also, buyers should expect fair separation from competitors: a car dealer spot should not run immediately after another competitive dealership's ad.

Advertising costs are higher with demand, such as the holiday season in fourth quarter, which is the most expensive time of the year. First quarter is the least costly. Ad dollars spring back in second quarter and slump a little in third.

Some radio station formats are personality-driven or offer news and sports with opportunities for sponsorships or the use of station talent to promote products and services.

Media planning for radio looks at the appeal of formats, such as Top 40, to target audience by demographics, psychographics and geography. Negotiation is based on either a cost-per-thousand (CPM) or cost per percentage of audience (CPP). Sales reps send the equivalent of a rate card, called availabilities (or avails) in broadcast advertising, list of time blocks and asking prices with asking prices based upon buyers' target and chosen air dates (known as a flight) requirements. Generally, station management plans a set of lower rates to use during negotiation to gain larger shares of the budget, and finally, the lowest "walk away" rates for the toughest concession. Media buyers continue discussions with sales staff as the schedule airs and afterward. In the event spots don't air as scheduled, buyers may accept or decline dates to reschedule. Unfair rotations and poor ratings as measured afterward may cause buyers to ask for free airings.

Stations use broadcast calendars that start on Mondays and many dayparts are listed as Monday through Friday or Monday through Sunday. Invoices are sent at the end of each broadcast month.

Creative spots are sent or trafficked to stations in time for approval and scheduling. Schedules may include several different versions of creative that are to be rotated or used at different dates.

Networks, local stations, syndicators and streaming programmers all have their own sales teams or representatives.

## Direct response radio

Lower rates from direct response rate cards not only mean spots air between broader time frames, but also, these purchases carry the risk of preemption, where other advertisers paying more get priority when inventory, the number of available slots, becomes tight. Preemption rates are somewhat predictable by seasonality or event (Olympics, sports playoffs, etc.), so risk mitigation is managed by advertisers willing to book more time to achieve their real goals. This process of overbooking, as it's called, carries more risk: that the entire amount of the contract will air. Still considered acceptable risks, direct response advertisers win by achieving an approximation of their original goals at lower prices.

Not every station has a direct response rate card. Generally, stations that don't simply offer ROS, or spot prices over broad time periods. Direct response radio can be managed closely, sometimes by getting air times after the fact within a few days, when stations have open inventory. Alternatively, stations may invoice twice a month, so buyers get a list of actual times that aired to calculate a true cost-per-order or cost-per-lead. With these calculations, called post-analysis, buyers can rebook time or renegotiate accordingly to try to improve results.

Using a tracking component is important to determine radio's effectiveness. Toll-free numbers and unique URLs are options as well as unique promo codes, such as a station's call letters, to attribute credit for leads and sales delivered by each facility's listeners and web site visitors.

The digital age also provides a significant visual component to radio with the addition of station web sites.

**Resources**

List of radio stations: http://www.radiolineup.com/

What Medium Scores Highest ROI? It May Be Radio:
http://adage.com/article/media/surprise-radio-beats-return-investment/292305

# Chapter 29

## Television

Traditional TV advertising is sold much like radio, by individual program and dayparts, using reach and frequency goals and CPP and/or CPM audience measurements.

Direct response television (DRTV), the least expensive method to start TV advertising, becomes performance-based with a call-to-action, by including a site link and/or toll-free number.

Many TV stations and network cable channels maintain a separate direct response rate card. Some require the call-to-action (CTA) functionality to earn these rates. Those that don't have a DRTV card will still probably sell time that rotates broadly, say from Monday-Sunday 6AM-2AM. As with all direct response methods, preemption is always a risk.

Length formats for television include ten, fifteen, thirty and sixty-second as well as two-minute, known as short-form commercials, and the 28:30 infomercial, or long-form version. The five-minute format is used infrequently. Fifteen and thirty-second are the most popular for traditional broadcast. Sixty-second is used most often in DRTV.

### What it takes to have a successful DRTV ad campaign
Keys to DRTV success include a good initial configuration of what will be offered to the consumer, a TV commercial that does a good job of demonstrating benefits and features, an overall excellent perceived value and strong call-to-action, telemarketing and fulfillment that are timely and efficient, and media buying that hits or beats the client's cost-per-order goal.

### Offer configuration
The costs of DRTV campaigns have driven marketers to build packages of products to increase their revenue per customer. Once a customer calls to order a product on the commercial, they may be asked about

purchasing several additional items, called upsells, during the call, up to four total, the ceiling for customer call fatigue. Sometimes the offer may include a second unit of the initial product and/or other related products, or others such as travel or discount clubs. The more closely related the upsell (additional purchase), the easier the sale.

The financial scenarios are examined in worksheets to determine which configuration makes the most sense. One measure of success is the ratio of sales to media expenditures. A media test of $20,000 that returns $40,000 in revenue yields a 2:1 and normally would proceed to a rollout phase, ramping up expenditures to expand to additional networks and stations. The final financial plan, total costs and allowed profit per unit subtracted from the retail price, determines the target cost-per-order for the campaign.

Critical to success is to hire DRTV professional services for each of these areas:
1. TV Production
It's best to choose experienced DRTV producers who know what it takes to get action either by phone calls or Internet. Commercials made by traditional agencies are often too soft, focusing on branding rather than a strong call-to-action.

2. Media Buying
DRTV buyers have proprietary databases with priceless data, including results by client for every time period purchased on each station and network. These pros also have commitments for ad time in the future to secure the best rates. Novices trying to buy time without this kind of history never get past a test because the prices they pay are too high. The greatest production would never get a fair chance to perform successfully.

3. Telemarketing
Pros in DRTV guide advertisers to write the tightest telemarketing scripts, provide the most accurate and daily overnight reporting so media buyers can evaluate expenditures and optimize the campaign.

4. Fulfillment
Shipping and customer service need to be handled by pros who know the timeliness of DRTV campaigns and are used to ramping up to be responsive to big rollout ad budgets. Customer service needs to be on the top of its game to protect the client's credit card processing privileges, for instance, by preventing chargebacks, or disputed transactions.

**TV production**
DRTV commercials are made in 60-second (:60), :120 and :30 lengths. A ballpark price to have one commercial in these three lengths is approximately $30,000. Variables include film vs. videotape, the number of locations, talent fees, etc. It makes sense to shoot enough to get the three versions for the increased placement with minimal extra in expenditure.

The timeframe from conception to completion is about eight weeks. The process includes scripting, shooting, editing with approvals. From the master tape, submasters are made, each with a different phone number so that sales can be determined by TV station. Phone numbers can be reused within 500 miles. For instance, an 800 number in Seattle can be used in Atlanta, which is obviously more than 500 miles away, for the most accurate tracking results. Network cable and regional networks all get their own phone numbers. It takes about 50 phone numbers (therefore about 50 submasters maximum) to run a good-sized campaign. From submasters, duplicate copies, or dubs, are sent to each station and network.

After testing over a short time frame, approximately two weeks, about half of all professionals tweak their commercial spots, making changes to try to improve results. Usually the hiatus between test and rollout, the continued, gradual increase in media expenditures, is about two weeks to make the changes in creative and schedule.

## TV media buying
Optimization is the key to success after a successful test.

Media buyers build an initial test from $5000-$20,000 to get a take on the strength of the commercial. They usually load tests with their strongest performing time periods for the product category and less expensive time slots than might be found later in a strong rollout.

Tests usually run over a 1-2-week period and analysis of results can be done daily during the test with a complete review the first business day after test completion. A general rule of thumb is that tests with a 2:1 ratio, or better, of revenues to media dollars spent, proceed to rollout.

In rollout, media expenditures start by rebooking all the winners from the test, possibly adding new time periods on the performing stations. In the markets of success, additions known to perform for the product category are added to testing each week. Optimization occurs by the weekly evaluation of results of each time slot that aired. Budgets are ramped up with continued success and approvals. The most successful campaigns may spend $250,000 per week. Keep in mind, they don't ramp up that high unless they hit the required ROI each week.

Seasonality is a consideration in planning a campaign. Fourth quarter is the most expensive, as clients are competing with the Christmas inventory pressure and ratings are their highest. Second quarter is the next most expensive. One of the problems with second quarter is that the audience is outside in warmer weather and the stations increase prices expecting DRTV advertisers to be like traditional ones who usually have strong Q2 budgets. Often DRTV media pros abstain from the big increases in pricing the first few weeks of April until prices drop to payout range. Third quarter may be the most profitable for some clients, being less expensive during a period of reruns. First quarter has high viewing levels due to winter weather, and TV stations charge the least, as traditional clients take hiatus.

Obviously, there is a seasonality to products as well. First quarter is great for resolutions, weight loss, stop-smoking, and fitness products. Fourth quarter is a great time to run spots for Christmas gifts, but the end of third quarter is the best time to test while rates are lower, leaving enough time to tweak creative before the fourth quarter campaign rollout.

A test media plan for $20,000 with an average $100 cost per spot would only have 200 airings across 10 different networks/stations. It is not unusual for spots to be bumped or removed from schedules and given to clients paying more money per spot.

Traditional advertisers pay greater prices to ensure their campaigns run during certain dates and time periods. DRTV advertisers are willing to be bumped, or preempted, to use the lower rates for campaign efficiency. Rates for DRTV also include broader time periods. Instead of running during late night programming between 1130PM and 1AM, the spots may be sold to run between the broader time range of 1130PM and 2AM.

DRTV clients rarely supplement their buy with time slots in prime time or news, due to the high price, which never generates the expected ROI. The higher the ratings, the greater the cost. It might be a choice made, say if the advertiser were an interview guest, for instance, understandably not made for efficiency.

Do not be surprised to see Monday-Sunday rotations between 2AM and 6AM on your media schedule. Just because you would never watch TV in the wee hours, don't forget that insomniacs and shift workers are everywhere. More importantly, success comes down to the price paid vs. the sales generated. The price for time after 2AM is very low. It may not take many sales to make the time period successful.

All late-night inventory is valuable to the DRTV advertiser. From about the time the phones in the household get quiet and kids go to bed, attention to DRTV creative increases.

**Local broadcast, syndicated and network television advertising**
Advertisers may choose to add local, or spot, market advertising to their DRTV schedule to choose selective programming. The cost per rating point (CPP), or percentage of the target audience reached, will be higher. DRTV rate cards do not sell any time in prime time. It can be worth it to sell to the right audience. The case I have always made is that you can hit your reach and frequency targets with a mix of dayparts. You don't need to step up to the cost of prime time. Unless, of course, it is part of a coordinated cross-promotion.

Syndicated programming offers the benefits of a given audience whether the show airs on or off a network. The Dr. Oz Show, for instance, is available from Sony Pictures ad sales.

The five major U.S. broadcast TV networks don't offer direct response rates and are the most expensive and each have their own sales teams. Audience sizes for network TV may be on the decline, but ad costs are going up. It's estimated that the average cost for prime time shows in fourth quarter 2019 will go up 10%.

**Resources**
Find broadcasters by market or by city:
https://www.nabonlineresourceguide.org/index.asp

Find network cable and TV facilities http://www.thevab.com/network-directory/networks-by-parent-company-1

Local area cable facilities: http://www.thevab.com/mvpd-directory

List of TV stations: http://www.stationindex.com/tv

# Chapter 30

## Monetize

Once your site and platforms begin to generate traffic, you can add methods to monetize visitor actions. You can: 1) allow Google to place ads of various sizes at different places of your choice on your site and/or 2) join affiliate programs as a publisher to choose and select appropriate ads to develop revenues relatively effortlessly.

### Google AdSense

While Google Ads is the advertiser's pay-per-click method to draw traffic, AdSense permits web sites to make money from Google Ads advertisers by allowing Google to place ads on their sites. An easy way to incorporate AdSense advertising for WordPress users is to select a plugin. Choose search or display ads that use text, video or images with links that will earn a payout which varies depending upon the format. Google pays 68% of the advertiser's click price for content and 51% for search. Google also pays for ads that lead to YouTube, as well as ads on the DoubleClick ad network.

Google looks at site traffic and content when approving prospects. Clearly, setting up the account, implementing the ad tracking code and learning about Google's rules will take some effort. These revenues are a relatively easy reward to sites for creating valuable content that appeals to a growing audience.

### Affiliate program: become a publisher

Advertisers create affiliate programs to find sites to run ads for them. It's easy to become one of those sites, called publishers. Affiliate networks, such as CJ Affiliate or ShareASale, provide platforms, basically catalogs of advertisers' ads, to monitor publisher performance and pay for results. Prospective publishers simply sign up, pull ads with tracking links to post on their sites. Posting ads requires more effort than setting up AdSense to run ads on a site, however choosing individual advertisers and ads may be worth the trouble. Both activities are worthwhile. Results are online 24/7. Some advertisers prefer to approve sites before allowing them to run their ads, called manual approval, but if the category fit is right, that should go smoothly.

In general, publishers make an average of 10% per sale. Each advertiser's profile shows previous offer performance so publishers can evaluate each one. Cost-per-sale requires more of the visitor, beyond the impression, click or engagement. Site real estate is valuable, so reviewing reports each month may lead to improved ad placement and higher revenues.

Like Google AdSense, becoming a publisher takes a little time to set up, but a site with decent traffic could generate significant revenues for a minimal investment in time, earning what I call money while you sleep. Affiliate marketing is performance marketing at its best: paying a portion of sales is a risk-free channel and one every marketer should embrace.

### Advertisers: become an affiliate
I recommend that every publisher investigate becoming an affiliate. One, this creates a new revenue stream by using your web assets to promote products/services you'd like to endorse. Two, publishers see first-hand what affiliates see, including competitor campaigns. Advertisers can tune into the EPC, or earnings-per-click measurement each merchant earns, a metric that calculates the average of its affiliate earnings divided by the number of clicks required.

### Content platforms
Medium offers a site where your posts can earn you money when they are viewed and reviewed by others.
Patreon offers a private, member-only platform where your subscribers pay for access to your content.
Kujabi is one of many course platforms where content delivers revenues.
Outbrain is another that will distribute your content to websites for free or payment.

These are just some of the many ways to monetize your assets.

**Further reading**

Making money with Google AdSense:
https://www.google.com/adsense/start/resources/making-money-with-google-adsense.html

Google AdSense Start: https://www.google.com/adsense/start/

Google payouts for AdSense advertising:
https://support.google.com/adsense/answer/180195?hl=en

Various metrics for payouts:
https://support.google.com/adsense/answer/6157433

Affiliate networks:
  Conversant: cj.com
  ShareASale.com

# Conclusion

If you haven't rushed to start promoting, but have done the appropriate basic planning, created sufficient content to cover your initial chosen channels and continue to generate a steady stream of valuable, engaging messages, your free and paid promotion efforts should yield the required leads over time.

The best results won't happen overnight. It will take some patience. The return on the investment of time and money should continue to improve overall. You should begin to realize maximum impact for minimal efforts. Continually test, tweak and repeat. Monitor and evaluate results regularly.

Each time you start a new channel, expect that the first week or month will be your worst performance until you begin to get results, make changes and improve returns. The more messages, the quicker you can get enough data to make decisions to get things going in the right direction. Have the patience to change one thing at a time so you can determine what makes the difference.

Check out Dmcenter.com to follow my latest recommendations, share yours and ask questions.

# Resources

I feel the same way that SEO expert Brendan does. That is why I wrote this book. I want to continue to share my best resources. Unfortunately, I can't share them all here and I keep adding new ones. Additionally, resources listed here may not be right for every situation. Check out Dmcenter.com to see more.

## Resources

| People to Follow | Free | |
|---|---|---|
| Denise Wakeman, Adventures in Visibility | URL Shortener | Bit.ly |
| Mari Smith, Facebook | Social media scheduler | Buffer, Later |
| Copyblogger | RSS feed aggregator | The Old Reader |
| Problogger | Graphic design & images | Canva |
| Seth Godin | Images | Pixabay, Unsplash, Pexels |
| Neil Patel | | |
| | **Services** | |
| **Marketing Newsletters** | Affiliate networks | ShareASale, Conversant |
| eMarketer | Sales tax software | Avalara |
| Marketing Profs | Fulfillment | Moulton Logistics |
| Social Media Examiner | Telemarketing | Direct Marketing Partners |
| Marketing Sherpa | Digital marketing | Beasley Direct |
| | | |
| **Recommended reading** | **Associations** | |
| Everybody Writes by Ann Handley | BBB | Better Business Bureau |
| SEO: Get Found Now: Search Engiine Optimizations Secrets | IAB | Internet Advertising Bureau |
| Local Search: Get Found Now: Local Search Secrets | ERA | Electronic Retailing Associaion |
| Twitter: The Definitive Twitter Guide | NRF | National Retail Federation |
| FTC Guidelines for Blogger Disclosure | Digital Commerce 360 | |
| FTC Advertising Rules | PDMI | Performance-driven Marketing Institute |
| CAN SPAM Law | | |
| PCI Data Security Standard | | |
| BBB Sample Privacy Policy | | |
| HIPAA Privacy and Security Rules | | |

Disclosure: I may receive compensation should you click through links from this book where I share products and services. In general, I share resources that I've used or vetted for clients or those recommended by colleagues.

# Appendices

## Appendix A: Competitive Statistics

| Competitive Statistics - Top Line | | | | | | | |
|---|---|---|---|---|---|---|---|
| Company | Revenues | Customers | Products | Offers | Employees | Credentials | Email Subscribers |

Competitive Statistics - Web and Social Stats

| | Web Site | | | | | | | | Social Statistics | | | | | | |
|---|---|---|---|---|---|---|---|---|---|---|---|---|---|---|---|
| Company (URL) | Global Rank | US Rank | Category Rank | Category | Keywords | Time on Site | Pages Viewed | Backlinks | Twitter followers | Facebook likes | YouTube views | Instagram followers | LinkedIn | Google+ | Pinterest |

# Appendix B: Content Inventory

Content Inventory Template

| Type | Inventory # | Date Created or Acquired (MM.DD.YY) | Description | Location | Use | Location URL | Size | DPI | Format | File size | License | Live (MM.D D.YY) | Alt Tag | Catego ry | Keyword s | Views | Subs | Original Source | Original Location | Original Title | Cost | P.O. |
|---|---|---|---|---|---|---|---|---|---|---|---|---|---|---|---|---|---|---|---|---|---|---|
| Digital asset | 101 | | Twitter backgn | Dropbox | Twitter account | https://www | 1600x900 px | | jpg | | | | | | | | | | | | | | |
| Logo | 102 | | Generic | Dropbox | Site home pag | http://www | 300x300 px | | png | | | | | | | | | | | | | | |
| Article | 103 | | Topic/author/e | Xyz site | MM Title: "How to... | http://www | 1500 words | | pdf | | | | | | | | | | | | | | |
| Video | 104 | | Elevator pitch | You Tube | Embed on site | http://www | 30 min. | | mp4 | | | | | | | | | | | | | | |
| Podcast | 105 | | Topic 1 | SoundCloud | Title: "3 Things | link | 30 min. | | mp3 | | | | | | | | | | | | | | |
| Product image | 106 | | Book 1 cover | Dropbox | Catalog | MM/Y"link | 150x241 px | | eps | | | | | | | | | | | | | | |
| Review | 107 | | Book 1 Review | Dropbox | Ad 1 | link | | | doc | | | | | | | | | | | | | | |
| Press | 108 | | Book quoted | Publication | Blog post 1 | link | | | doc | | | | | | | | | | | | | | |
| Image | 109 | | Question mark | Pixabay | Blog post 1 | link | 500x500 px | | jpg BW | | | | | | | | | | | | | | |
| Brochure | 110 | | Trifold - service | Dropbox | 2017-2018 | link | 8 1/2x11 | | pdf | | | | | | | | | | | | | | |
| Release | 111 | | Book 1 launch | Wire Service | Landing page | link | 500 words | | pdf | | | | | | | | | | | | | | |
| Interview | 112 | | Book 1 launch | XYZ Radio | Blog post 1 | link | 60 min. | | mp3 | | | | | | | | | | | | | | |
| Whitepaper | 113 | | Topic 2 | Site | Download | link | 15 pages | | pdf | | | | | | | | | | | | | | |
| Case study | 114 | | | Dropbox | | link | | | pdf | | | | | | | | | | | | | | |
| Testimonial | 115 | | | Dropbox | | link | | | doc | | | | | | | | | | | | | | |

Article
Blog post
Brochure
Case study
Digital asset
Image
Interview
Logo
Podcast
Press
Product image
Release
Review
Testimonial
Video
Whitepaper

154

# Appendix C: Image Inventory

The image inventory template helps to manage a growing library of assets. Create a number for each version, document its origin, license, cost, method and location of use. Add or remove columns to customize the template to your needs.

1) **Inventory number** – Track each asset across internal activities with a unique identifier. Use your naming convention consistently.
2) **Name** – Create a simple, new name or use the original name. Keep in mind that each field should help to locate the asset easily.
3) **Type** – The template includes a drop-down list with a sampling of types of images from which to choose. The list, in sheet 2 called Types, is meant to be altered.
4) **Description** – Make sure you can find it fast. Capsulize and distinguish each image from others succinctly.
5) **Source** – Whether the asset was created in-house or acquired elsewhere, record the author or original location.
6) **Acquired or created date** – Log the date each asset is obtained or produced to document evidence of rights.
7) **Original link** – If the item is purchased, copy the link for reference, which is helpful to collect another version or provide proof of derivation.
8) **Size** – Refer to a physical size, such as pixels, inches or feet.
9) **File size** – This field helps when choosing an asset or resizing it for use.
10) **DPI** – A DPI record reveals resolution that may or may not be appropriate for use.
11) **Format** – A drop-down menu here can provide a catalog of choices: PDF, JPG, PNG, etc. for selection appropriate to its purpose.
12) **Cost** – This field is useful to locate the cost of one or sorting several over a fixed period for accounting and budgeting.
13) **P.O.** – When purchase orders are required, this field associates an asset with the expense.
14) **License** – While images may be obtained for free, it's important to document the kind of license to comply with copyright restrictions. CreativeCommons.org, for instance, provides a variety of choices to content creators that address attribution, sharing, modifying or reuse for
15) **Renewal date** – Record deadline to pay any renewal fees. Note: calendar a task to thirty days prior to renewal for permission requests.
16) **Use** – Create a drop-down for this column to list the assortment of placements, e.g. ad, banner stand, brochure, blog post, trade show booth, or website.
17) **Posted date** – Catalog the date that the asset is published, whether physically, as in a poster, or digitally, as in a social media background.
18) **Live URL** – Register the URL, if applicable, where the asset is posted.
19) **Storage location** – List where the item is stored, whether in a file cabinet, computer folder or URL in the cloud, complete with folder hierarchy.
20) **Removal date** – Document the date that the asset was unpublished or the materials become obsolete.
21) **Alt tag** – These tags help the visually impaired and those that block image downloads to know what is in the image. Tags and titles also help gain search engine juice. Record with asset for reference.
22) **Alt titles** – Provides further concise, catchy information about the image and should be stored with information about the asset.
23) **Keywords** – Unlike keywords for search marketing, keywords in an image inventory should help internal staff locate the asset quickly. Choose keywords thoughtfully, keeping in mind related assets.

Keeping this log up-to-date is important and worthwhile to save time and unwanted trouble.

Image Inventory Template

155

# Appendix D: Editorial Calendar

## Editorial Calendar--Events

| January | February | March | April | May | June | July | August | September | October | November | December |
|---|---|---|---|---|---|---|---|---|---|---|---|
| New Year's resolution Article | New product White paper | Personnel announcement | Trade show Co-author article announcement Article | White paper | Update announcement | Article | White paper Industry legislation | Trade show | Article | White paper | Holiday |

## Editorial Calendar--Content

| Month | January | February | March | April | May | June | July | August | September | October | November | December |
|---|---|---|---|---|---|---|---|---|---|---|---|---|
| | Newsletter | Newsletter 2 | Newsletter 3 | Newsletter 4 | Newsletter 5 | Newsletter | Newsletter | Newsletter 8 | Newsletter 9 | Newsletter 10 | Newsletter 11 | Newsletter 12 |
| | Cont | Whitepaper 1 | | Trade show | Whitepaper 2 | | | Whitepaper 3 | Trade show 2 | | Whitepaper 4 | |
| | Emailing | Emailing | Emailing | Emailing | Emailing | Emailing | Emailing | Emailing | Emailing | Emailing | Emailing | Holiday email |
| | New Year's email | | Show release | Show release 2 | | | | | Show release | Show release 2 | | |
| | | | Show email 1 | Show email | Show email 3 | | | | Show email 1 | Show email 2 | Show email 3 | |
| | Article | | | Article | | | Article | | | Article | | |
| | Social media | Social media | Social media | Social media | Social media | Social media | Social media | Social media | Social media | Social media | Social media | Social media |

## Content Assignment Calendar

| Publication | Publish date | Due date | Author(s) | Topic/Title | Goals/Description | Target | Offer(s) | Keywords | Hashtags | Image |
|---|---|---|---|---|---|---|---|---|---|---|
| | | | | | | | | | | |

# Appendix E: Benchmarks

## Marketing Benchmarks - Summary

| | YTD Sales | | YTD Leads | | Call Center | | Website | |
|---|---|---|---|---|---|---|---|---|
| | # Sales | % of Goal | # Leads | % of Goal | # Leads | # Sales | # Leads | # Sales |
| Week ending MM/DD/YY | | | | | | | | |

## Marketing Benchmarks - Core Assets

| | Website | | | | | | | | Blog | | | Podcast | | |
|---|---|---|---|---|---|---|---|---|---|---|---|---|---|---|
| | Total Site Visits | Unique Site Visits | Global Rank | U.S. Rank | Category Rank | Visit Duration | Pages/ Visit | # Backlinks | Cart Abandon- ment | Visitors | Duration | Pages/ Visit | Episode | # Listen ers | Cost per Order |
| Week ending MM/DD/YY | | | | | | | | | | | | | | |

## Marketing Benchmarks - Email and Press

| | Emails | | | | | Press Releases | | | | Articles/Ads | |
|---|---|---|---|---|---|---|---|---|---|---|---|
| | Bulk Emails | Subscribers / Audience | Opens | ClickThru/ Opens | Conversions | # | Views | Posts | Clicks to Site | Number | Circulation |
| Week ending MM/DD/YY | | | | | | | | | | | |

## Marketing Benchmarks - Social Media (Free)

| | Twitter | | | | | Facebook | | | | | YouTube | | | | | |
|---|---|---|---|---|---|---|---|---|---|---|---|---|---|---|---|---|
| | Tweets | Followers | Retweets/ Mentions | Audience | Likes | Views | Likes | Followers | Reach | Engagements | Subscribers | Views | Unique | Views | Likes | Comments | Shares |
| Week ending MM/DD/YY | | | | | | | | | | | | | | | | |

## Marketing Benchmarks - Social Media (Free)

| | Pinterest | | | | | Foursquare | | | |
|---|---|---|---|---|---|---|---|---|---|
| | Followers | Pins | Repins | Likes | Comments | Followers | Likes | Tips | Shares | Lists |
| Week ending MM/DD/YY | | | | | | | | | |

## Marketing Benchmarks - Digital Paid

| | Pay Per Click | | | | | Affiliate Program | | | |
|---|---|---|---|---|---|---|---|---|---|
| | Cost | CTR | CPC | Sales | CPO | Cost | CTR | CPC | Sales | CPO |
| Week ending MM/DD/YY | | | | | | | | | |

## Marketing Benchmarks - Social Media Paid

| | Facebook | | | Instagram | | | Pinterest | | |
|---|---|---|---|---|---|---|---|---|---|
| | $ Spent | Audience (000) | CPO | $ Spent | Audience (000) | CPO | $ Spent | Audience (000) | CPO |
| Week ending MM/DD/YY | | | | | | | | | |

## Marketing Benchmarks - Traditional Offline Paid

| | Direct Mail | | | | | | | Print | | | | | |
|---|---|---|---|---|---|---|---|---|---|---|---|---|---|
| | $ Spent | # Mailed | Leads | Cost per Lead | # Orders | # Returns | Cost per Order | $ Spent | Circulation (000) | # Leads | Cost per Lead | # Orders | Cost per Order |
| Week ending MM/DD/YY | | | | | | | | | | | | | |

## Marketing Benchmarks - Traditional Offline Paid

| | Radio | | | | | | Television | | | | | |
|---|---|---|---|---|---|---|---|---|---|---|---|---|
| | $ Spent | Audience (000) | # Leads | Cost per Lead | # Orders | Cost per Order | % Spent | Audience | # Leads | Cost/Lead | # Orders | Cost/ Order |
| Week ending MM/DD/YY | | | | | | | | | | | | |

# Glossary

| Word | Definition |
|------|------------|
| acquiring bank | the merchant's financial institution for accepting credit card payments |
| AdSense | Google's ad-serving service for website owners to be paid for actions taken by their visitors |
| affiliate | a website that agrees to post ads seen by their visitors in exchange for agreed-upon payment, usually a percent of a sale |
| affiliate network | a software system that serves as a hub between advertisers and affiliate websites to calculate visitor actions and sales, pay affiliates and host ads |
| affiliate program | description, payout, product lists, images and unique linking system, reporting, customer service and payment method |
| air dates | chosen dates for live or recorded transmissions through radio, TV and digital facilities |
| allowable | the budget per product available to spend on advertising after costs |
| autoresponder | a preset email response programmed to be sent after a specific action by a web visitor |
| autoship | a method to schedule purchases that recur periodically, often monthly, also known as contiuity programs |
| availabilities (avails) | inventory of dates and time slots available for advertising, notably of radio and TV facilities |

| | |
|---|---|
| B2B | a sales and marketing model to sell business-to-business |
| B2C | a sales and marketing model to sell business-to-consumer |
| backlinks | links that send traffic to a website |
| benchmark | point of reference, used to measure improvements in analytics |
| blog | a web page dedicated to multiple posts, usually less than 1500 words each |
| Brand Ambassador | paid endorser, such as an influencer |
| branding | marketing efforts to increase awareness and create a household name for a company or person |
| bump | when a commercial or ad is preempted |
| CAN SPAM | Pornography And Marketing Act of 2003, businesses must comply with to identify company sending email and allow opt-out unsubscription |
| cart abandonment | act of web visitor leaving a site without completing an order |
| category | a blogging feature to group posts together by topics |
| channel | individual station, cable facility or media channel |
| chargebacks | action taken by consumer to reverse a credit card charge |
| circulation | distribution of a publication by geography, such as county, metro, national or global |
| continuity program | sale of products or services on a recurring basis |
| conversion | action completed by prospect |
| CPA | cost-per-acquisition: cost to secure an action, lead or sale, such as capture a visitor's contact information |

| | |
|---|---|
| CPC | cost-per-click: cost to secure a web visitor's click through to a landing page |
| CPM | cost-per-thousand: cost to reach 1,000 audience members |
| CPO | cost-per-order: cost to secure a transaction |
| CPP | cost-per-point: cost to reach 1% of a target group |
| CPS | cost-per-sale: same as cost-per-order |
| CRM | customer relationship & contact management software |
| CTA | call-to-action: a marketing request designed to elicit a response |
| CTR | click-through rate: % of internet viewers who click on a link |
| CXO | used to describe any of several C-level positions as a group (CEO, COO, CFO, etc.) |
| D2C | another expression for B2C, a sales and marketing model to sell direct-to-consumer |
| data visualization | charting spreadsheet data to graphically decipher meaning, make decisions regarding future actions and changes |
| daypart | selected blocks of time during which commercials air for one rate within each range |
| deeplink | link to a specific page of a website rather than a home page |
| demographic | age and sex of a target audience |
| dimensional direct mail piece | mailings designed to capture attention with objects in addition to flat pieces |

| | |
|---|---|
| direct response | advertising integrated with mechanisms to elicit response, such as links or phone numbers |
| discount rate | the base rate charged to a merchant for payment processing services on debit and credit card transactions |
| discovery | in marketing, the process to determine a company's needs, challenges, and desired results |
| display ad | non-classified ads in digital or print publications |
| double opt-in | functionality, such as email confirmation, to secure two confirmations of the same permission, such as a subscription |
| downsell | second product or service at a lower price than an initial offer that was declined |
| DRTV | direct response television uses broad time ranges at reduced rates and intended for consumer actions to go to site or call phone number |
| dubs | copies of master or submaster, generally shipped digitally |
| DUNS number | Dun and Bradstreet's Data Universal Numbering System to identify a business with a 9-digit code |
| EPC | Earnings Per Click an affiliate marketing term demonstrating the average earnings per click affiliates of a certain advertiser are receiving |
| Evergreen | in marketing, a description for content that has lasting value which may be referred to often in the future |
| flight | schedule of air dates between start and finish of a campaign |
| frequency (R&F; print volume) | average number ot times an audience sees a campaign or message |

| | |
|---|---|
| Google Ads | Google's service to sell advertising on a pay-per-click model |
| Google Analytics | free measurement of site actions |
| Google Search Console | tools and reports measure site search traffic, performance and identify issues to fix |
| hashtag | word or words preceded by number sign used to search on topics and events |
| HIPAA | Health Insurance Portability and Accountability Act of 1996, data security and privacy protection to safeguard individual medical information |
| inbound marketing | program of content that acquires traffic, leads and sales |
| inbound telemarketing | activities of live operators and marketing automation to collect information from callers |
| influencer | celebrity, blogger, podcaster or other individual with a loyal following |
| insertion order | contract for ad placement stipulating dates, position, sizes, formats, etc. |
| inventory | in media, available ad slots |
| issuing bank | in payment processing, the financial institution of the consumer credit instrument |
| IVR | Interactive voice response systems help marketers automatically collect information from callers through pre-programmed scripts and technology |
| keyword | word or phrase used to find results on websites |
| KPI | key performance indicator, a metric to track campaign performance, such as sales, clicks, leads, etc. |

| | |
|---|---|
| landing page | web pages designed to provide specific information promised by a previous message |
| long-form | in infomercials, the twenty-eight minute, thirty-second length |
| makegood | in media, a replacement for an ad not run, or not run correctly in date, placement due to preemption or error |
| manage preferences | a method for subscribers to opt-out and choose what emailings they subscribe to, usually present at the footer of email blasts |
| media plan | a comprehensive detail of objectives, target audience, strategies and tactics across geographies to designed to meet budget and other goals |
| medium | one chosen channel, such as radio or print |
| merchant | commonly used to describe an advertiser in an affiliate network |
| merchant ID | the payment processor representing card brands such as MasterCard and Visa, needed to process credit card transactions |
| meta description | up to 155 characters that describe the content of a page used by search engines in results |
| meta title | page title as visible in browser for both search engine robots and web visitors |
| metatag | HTML elements of a web page that are not readily visible and displayed as <meta> hidden in the code at the top of the page |
| milestone | an important stage in development |

| | |
|---|---|
| mind map | a data visualization, such as an organizational chart or steps in a process |
| Native ads | ads placed within editorial content that closely resemble the format of that content |
| network tv | U.S. group of company owned as well as affiliated local market broadcast stations, such as CBS, NBC and Fox. |
| offer configuration | a product or service with any other items packaged and priced together |
| optimization | efforts to improve results of a campaign, such as using keywords in search marketing on web pages to improve visibility, traffic and results |
| opt-in | a single selection of agreement, for instance to give permission to send an email newsletter |
| opt-out | selection to remove a name from a list |
| organic search | in search marketing, entering one or more words into a search engine yielding results at no charge to companies |
| outbound marketing | messages sent by organizations |
| outbound telemarketing | calls by operators and recordings automatically sent to prospects |
| overbook | act of buying more media than required to meet goals |
| payment processor | company between card brand, such as Visa, and an end-user merchant that provides the ability for the merchant to accept credit cards |
| payout | the fixed amount or percentage that an business allows its web site vendors and affiliates |

| | |
|---|---|
| PCI | industry rule requiring credit card merchants to protect consumer data and complete annual questionnaires and/or scans to show compliance |
| performance-based | marketing efforts built to generate response at a fixed price per action |
| permalinks | URL address for a web page including a domain followed by words used to find the content |
| pfishing | fraudulent practice of duping email recipients to reveal their personally identifiable information |
| PII | personally identifiable information to be protected in the U.S. and abroad |
| pixel | a small piece of code or measure of an image on a digital screen |
| plugins | a software component that adds a specific feature to an existing computer program, such connecting spam blocker to a WordPress blog |
| podcasting | audio recordings posted online |
| post-analysis | study of statistics to find areas for improvement and track success |
| PPC | pay-per-click: method of search marketing to fix a price per web visitor action to click on a link |
| preemption | removal of an ad from a schedule due to another advertiser paying more, breaking news event, program overrun or error |
| psychographic | combination of demographic, geographic, income and other information to create a lifestyle segment |
| publisher | a web site or print entity |

| | |
|---|---|
| radio station format | type of niche audience served, such as country & western, rock and roll and the like |
| rate cards | schedule of prices for media set on a sliding scale for volume and including special sections, sponsorship and combinations |
| rating point | 1% of any given target audience; used as a measure to buy TV time |
| reach | the percentage of an audience to receive a message |
| rebook | a commercial that is rescheduled after preemption |
| remarketing | pay-per-click and email methods to touch a prospect after one or more previous touches |
| remnant advertising | discounted media based on last-minute availability and pre-approved creative |
| repurposing | reusing all or part of content in one or more formats and/or platforms |
| reserve | funds held by payment processor, notably for high-risk merchant accounts |
| retargeting | pay-per-click method to touch a prospect after one or more previous touches |
| robocall | automated telephone call |
| rollout | ad schedule after successful testing which is gradually increased with continued success |
| ROS | Run-of-station allows the widest rotation of commercials, during anytime during the broadcast day or week |
| rotation | the placement of ads to be equally spaced out during a time period or for creatives to each get equal exposure |

| | |
|---|---|
| RSS feed | Really Simple Syndication, automatic delivery of blog or site content after subsription |
| run date | date an ad will air or publish |
| satellite | media channels available through satellite distribution, such as Sirius XM, DirecTV or Dish |
| search marketing | efforts to insert keywords into content and pay for visitors who click through search ads |
| SEM | search engine marketing includes both organic (free) and pay-per-click efforts |
| SEO | search engine optimization |
| short-form | in TV, commercials two-minutes or shorter in length |
| spot | a radio or TV commercial |
| spot tv | TV broadcast stations in local markets |
| streaming | web content delivered live or for immediate playback |
| submaster | in television, a copy of a commercial with a unique phone number and/or URL |
| suppression list | group of email addresses that have opted out and unsubscribed |
| SWOT | a strategic planning technique used by businesses to identify strengths, weaknesses, opportunities and threats |
| syndication | newspaper, broadcast |
| tags | word or words used to label and identify blog topics and images, for instance |
| target audience | the segment of an audience whether geographic, demographic or psychographic for given campaigns and messages |

| | |
|---|---|
| tear sheet | a physical page of a magazine or newspaper proving an ad was published; may be emailed as a PDF file |
| terrestrial | description of radio or TV stations using over-the-air broadcast signals |
| touch | one message to a prospect |
| tracking pixel | a small piece of code added to a web page to identify, count and credit actions |
| underwriting | in payments, the processor staff who review applications to accept credit card payments |
| Unique Selling Proposition | known as USP or unique value proposition, |
| unsubscribe | the act to remove from a subscription, such as to an email newsletter or print publication |
| upfront | in network TV time buying, the period when new fall primetime shows are previewed and sold, around May |
| upsell | upon completion of an order, an additional order, usually the same price or less |
| URL | Uniform Record Locator or web address |
| vanity number | a toll-free number with digits that spell our one or more words |

# Author Bio

ROI-driven, Jan Carroza helps clients make the right decisions when developing marketing strategies and choosing channels. An early adopter, she enjoys studying and sharing new opportunities and ways to optimize efforts. Her multi-sided career spans agency, advertiser, audience research, media, mobile and privacy software experience. While her background in multichannel campaign management began in traditional advertising (print, radio and TV), performance-based marketing inspires her in-house mentality to achieve the maximum return-on-investment for clients.

As a trainer of customers, students and staff in direct response, media planning, mobile and privacy SaaS solutions, Jan realizes the importance to educate prospects to earn trust. Previous clients include: M&M Mars, Volvo, Time-Life, Soloflex, Blue Cross, Braun, Sears, Peninsula Hotels, Kemper Financial Services and American Express.

She has spoken to groups at retail, privacy and media conventions and taught Media Planning at Pepperdine University's Malibu campus. She earned her B.A. in Radio/TV at SIU/Edwardsville.

# Endorsements

"There has never been a time when I've turned to Jan that she hasn't been able to answer to the most complex marketing challenge. Jan is the best at keeping up with marketing trends, constantly being curious about new technologies and strategies that are converting, and remembering the basics that are still relevant today! This book is true marketing magic."

Lauryn Wingate
The Devereux Group, a professional business consultancy

"Jan Carroza knows more about how to make an eCommerce business successful than anyone I know. She looks at a business from every angle: operations, marketing, merchandising, and distribution … and figures out the right products at the right price and how to market them profitably. Her book is a "must read" for anyone contemplating an eCommerce business or who is running one and needs to do it better."

Laurie Beasley
President, Beasley Direct and Online Marketing, Inc.
President, Direct Marketing Association of Northern California

"Jan Carroza is a wonderful community builder and leader, as well as a lead generation expert, a pro with advanced promotions, media, and campaigns. I've learned a ton from her about sharing and community strategies. Jan has a wealth of knowledge and is the best kind of mentor because she gives you what you need at just the right time. I highly recommend working with Jan for any sales conversion program."

Cynthia Trevino
SheMarketsMentor.com

"I have worked with Jan for over 25 years in various capacities…co-workers, client/vendor and vendor/client relationships. She never ceases to amaze me with her knowledge of the e-commerce world. She has exceptional marketing prowess, superior technical aptitude and the demeanor of a caring teacher. Her curiosity for learning is admirable which is only surpassed by her ability to comprehend new marketing technologies and how to successfully apply them."

Kathy Kelly
Kathy Kelly Productions, Inc. & Kathy Kelly Photography